The Bible Adventure Book of Scavenger Hunts

Kelly Anne White

ISBN: 978-1-60679-355-8
Library of Congress Control Number: 2016933830
Book layout: Cheery Sugabo
Cover design: Cheery Sugabo
Front cover photo: oliveromg/Shutterstock.com

Healthy Learning
P.O. Box 1828
Monterey, CA 93942
www.healthylearning.com

Dedication

I dedicate this book with love to Mimi, who showed me that a gal can camp out, stoke a fire, cast a fishing line, and still wear crimson-color lipstick…even if it smudges.

Acknowledgment

Dear God,

A ring of fire dances behind the trees
Then floats up and reveals itself
A mirror ball that holds no secrets
But radiates truth not manifested yet

A puff of thick white smoke
Provides the pillowy framework
For a story that shifts
To the right of the moonlight

An eagle spreads its wings
To take off in flight
And seamlessly melts into the sky
As it finds its freedom within

A ram so strong and determined
Bursts through a cloud
Its majestic horns
Gyrating into eternity

The Anointed One steps into the night
And wraps a painted blanket
Around our burning desires
So all can see the beauty in the darkness

Love, Kelly

Contents

One-With-Nature Hike
Strap on the hiking boots—it's time to head for the woods and hit the trails!

Name Guessing Game
Discover "who's who" in your group *and* in biblical times.
   Hello, my name is...

Garden of Seedin'
Dig gardening? Good thing since this search gets down to the real dirt.

Search for Your Supper
Hungry, anyone? Not so fast! First, some hunting and gathering...

Lost and Found
What goes up must come down. What gets lost must be found.

Raiders of Noah's Ark
Animals are supposed to board the ark in pairs, right?
   Noah needs help, matey!

Quotes of Many Colors
Even if the sky is drab and dreary, this colorful activity brightens any day.

Introduction

Are you ready to embark on some brand-new adventures based on old-school biblical themes? Great—round up the kids and teens! *The Bible Adventure Book of Scavenger Hunts* is jam-packed with loads of fun activities created around scripture verses—all quoted from the New International Version (NIV).

The book features not only scavenger hunts, but also craft projects, easy recipes, science experiments, and other elements, with each chapter highlighting a specific Bible theme. Following are some points to be mindful of when planning *The Bible Adventure Book of Scavenger Hunts* activities:

- *The scavenger hunts in this book are terrific for summer camps,* youth groups, campground coordinators, homeschooling programs, vacation Bible school, family gatherings, church events, and even birthday parties.

- *Most of the activities can be completed with any number of players,* and leaders can organize for teams, pairs, or individuals accordingly. Plus, there's something in here for kids of all ages.

- *Read all of the game and project instructions carefully* and thoroughly before planning any activity since many have particular nuances. Almost all of the scavenger hunts require some preparation, such as hiding clues and other items.

- *No time for prep? All of the scavenger activities contain other elements*—fill-in-the-blanks, science projects, color-by-symbols—that can be completed independent of the hunts. Most also include easy-to-photocopy handouts.

- *The best characteristic of these scavenger hunts is that they can be fine-tuned* to fit into any schedule or landscape. Detailed instructions and clues are provided, so give each game your own twist to kick off a scavenger-hunt tradition within your group or family.

- *There's only one rule that's set in stone,* and it applies to all of this book's hunts and other activities: *Have fun with it!*

CHAPTER 1
One-With-Nature Hike

Since the creation of the world God's invisible qualities—his eternal power and divine nature—have been clearly seen.

Romans 1:20

One-With-Nature Hike

What better way to kick off a scavenger hunt book than with a nature theme that emphasizes God's love for our beautiful earth? Scripture references drive the game, inspiring players to search for natural bounty (like leaves and feathers) along wooded areas and hiking trails. Players can go out in groups, or pair off, depending on safety issues. Before the trailblazing begins, on the opposite page are a few ground rules for players. Photocopy this list of rules to hand out along with scavenger lists, which appear on pages that follow.

omgimages/Thinkstock

The Bible Adventure Book of Scavenger Hunts

One-With-Nature Hike Ground Rules

- *Photograph some list items,* rather than collecting, since many elements of nature—wild animals in particular—need to be left undisturbed. It's also best to snap pictures of plants that are potentially poisonous or with thorns.

- *Please have adult supervision* during this nature excursion, of course, as well as for other hunts in this book.

- *Bring along backpacks* for hauling loot, and remember to toss in healthful snacks and bottles of water for hydration.

- *Other containers are useful* for stowing items like rocks and grass in backpacks. Choose from small plastic tubs with lids, plastic zip-top bags, or lightweight baby food jars (see Jarheads project on the following page).

- *Take disposable shopping bags* for picking up litter spotted along the way. Hang on to trash that could be turned to "treasures," such as old fishing lures or cool bottle caps (nothing too sharp or rusty, please), for the Nature's Hang-up hanging-mobile project at the end of this chapter.

- *Use nature-lovin' discretion*—only pluck a wildflower, for example, if there is an abundance of them. Otherwise, snap a picture, and leave the flower to thrive in its natural habitat. Collect natural items even if not on the scavenger list—for example, a pretty pinecone to hang on your mobile.

- *Gather only what has fallen* to the ground when looking for things such as bird feathers and tree bark. Removing bark from a tree can weaken its defense against insects and disease.

Craft Fun! Jarheads

Used baby food jars are the best for stashing small stuff like seeds and dust, or bugs and worms. Be kind to crawly creatures, providing a comfortable temporary home and setting them free afterward.

moodboard/Thinkstock

What you need: baby food jars, masking tape (various shades of tan and green), nail or knife

1) Clean and dry the jars (you can do this with small plastic containers, too).
2) Cut or tear masking tape into small scraps and shapes.
3) Place pieces of tape around outsides of jars to decorate in a camouflage pattern.
4) If using jars to collect bugs, carefully use the tip of a sharp knife or nail to poke holes in the lids and leave some clear spots on the jars as "windows" for light. Add a handful of grass and drops of water. Carry on!

Night-light!

At night, place lightning bugs in decorated jars. As the bugs light up, it creates a camo-pattern stained-glass effect. Remember to set them free before the night is out!

Ready for the Hunt

Give each player a list comprised of the Bible verses on the following pages, have them complete the fill-in-the-blanks to figure out the correct scavenger-hunt items, and send them on their way. Difficult-to-find items are grouped accordingly, so choose a preferred level of challenge. Or, mix-and-match to make your own list that's conducive to elements that are naturally indigenous to the area. (An answer key immediately follows the lists.)

lvdesign77/iStock/Thinkstock

The Bible Adventure Book of Scavenger Hunts

Biblical Fill-in-the-Blanks

Easiest

- The Lord is my _____, my fortress and my deliverer. 2 Samuel 22:2

- When you rebuke and discipline anyone for their sin, you consume their wealth like a _____—surely everyone is but a breath. Psalm 39:11

- He will cover you with his _____, and under his wings you will find refuge; his faithfulness will be your shield and rampart. Psalm 91:4

- Those who trust in their riches will fall, but the righteous will thrive like a green _____. Proverbs 11:28

- _____ are creatures of little strength, yet they store up their food in the summer. Proverbs 30:25

- I went down to the grove of _____ trees to look at the new growth in the valley. Song of Songs 6:11

- The _____ withers and the _____ fall, but the word of our God endures forever. Isaiah 40:8

- The _____ will devour them like wool. But my righteousness will last forever, my salvation through all generations. Isaiah 51:8

- Son of man, how is the wood of a _____ different from that of a _____ from any of the trees in the forest? Ezekiel 15:2

- She has heaped up silver like dust, and gold like the _____ of the streets. Zechariah 9:3

- But the _____ of the Spirit is love, joy, peace, forbearance, kindness, goodness, faithfulness, gentleness and self-control. Against such things there is no law. Galatians 5:22–23

The Bible Adventure Book of Scavenger Hunts

Biblical Fill-in-the-Blanks

Intermediate

- I will surely bless you and make your descendants as numerous as the stars in the sky and as the _____ on the seashore. Genesis 22:17

- Jacob took fresh-cut branches from poplar, almond and plane trees and made white stripes on them by peeling the _____ and exposing the white inner wood of the branches. Genesis 30:37

- All flying _____ are unclean to you; do not eat them. Leviticus 11:21

- Then he shall take some holy water in a _____ jar and put some _____ from the tabernacle floor into the _____. Numbers 5:17

- At the scent of water it will _____ and put forth shoots like a plant. Job 14:9

- When the _____ is removed and new growth appears and the grass from the hills is gathered in, the lambs will provide you with clothing and the goats with the price of a field. Proverbs 27:25–26

- A _____ can be caught with the hand, yet it is found in kings' palaces. Proverbs 30:28

- I am a _____ of Sharon, a _____ of the valleys. Song of Songs 2:1

- I will shake the people of Israel among all the nations as _____ is shaken in a sieve, and not a _____ will reach the ground. Amos 9:9

- If we have sown spiritual _____ among you, is it too much if we reap a material harvest from you? 1 Corinthians 9:11

- He spit on the ground, made some _____ with the saliva, and put it on the man's eyes. John 9:6

The Bible Adventure Book of Scavenger Hunts

Biblical Fill-in-the-Blanks

Advanced

- The _____ will leave you and your houses, your officials and your people; they will remain only in the Nile. Exodus 8:11

- You may eat any kind of _____, _____, _____ or _____. But all other flying insects that have four legs you are to regard as unclean. Leviticus 11:22–23

- He makes my feet like the feet of a _____; he causes me to stand on the heights. 2 Samuel 22:34

- Cleanse me with _____, and I will be clean; wash me, and I will be whiter than snow. Psalm 51:7

- There is nothing Egypt can do—head or tail, _____ branch or _____. Isaiah 19:15

- I am not angry. If only there were _____ and _____ confronting me! I would march against them in battle; I would set them all on fire. Isaiah 27:4

- He cut down _____, or perhaps took a _____ or _____. He let it grow among the trees of the forest, or planted a _____, and the rain made it grow. Isaiah 44:14

- The Son of Man will send out his angels, and they will _____ out of his kingdom everything that causes sin and all who do evil. Matthew 13:41

- They pursued it not by faith but as if it were by works. They stumbled over the stumbling _____. Romans 9:32

- If the part of the dough offered as firstfruits is holy, then the whole batch is holy; if the _____ is holy, so are the branches. Romans 11:16

- Spread out above the heads of the living creatures was what looked something like a vault, sparkling like _____, and awesome. Ezekiel 1:22

Answer Key: Biblical Fill-in-the-Blanks

These are the answers for the Biblical Fill-in-the-Blanks handouts (on previous pages). If you need a quicker game or have a younger group, simply use this answer key as the scavenger list and perhaps plan a group discussion later to address each item's relevant scripture.

Easiest

- rock (2 Samuel 22:2)
- moth (Psalm 39:11)
- feathers (Psalm 91:4)
- leaf (Proverbs 11:28)
- ants (Proverbs 30:25)
- nut (Song of Songs 6:11)
- grass, flowers (Isaiah 40:8)
- worm (Isaiah 51:8)
- vine, branch (Ezekiel 15:2)
- dirt (Zechariah 9:3)
- fruit (Galatians 5:22–23)

Intermediate

- sand (Genesis 22:17)
- bark (Genesis 30:37)
- insects (Leviticus 11:21)
- clay, dust, water (Numbers 5:17)
- bud (Job 14:9)
- hay (Proverbs 27:25–26)
- lizard (Proverbs 30:28)
- rose, lily (Song of Songs 2:1)
- grain, pebble (Amos 9:9)
- seed (1 Corinthians 9:11)
- mud (John 9:6)

Advanced

- frogs (Exodus 8:11)
- locust, katydid, cricket, grasshopper (Leviticus 11:22–23)
- deer (2 Samuel 22:34)
- hyssop (Psalm 51:7)
- palm, reed (Isaiah 19:15)
- briers, thorns (Isaiah 27:4)
- cedars, cypress, oak, pine (Isaiah 44:14)
- weed (Matthew 13:41)
- stone (Romans 9:32)
- root (Romans 11:16)
- crystal* (Ezekiel 1:22)

*Science-savvy kids will know to search not only for semiprecious crystal gems such as natural quartz and garnet, but also common crystals like ice, salt, and sugar.

lvdesign77/iStock/Thinkstock

Fun for Word Nerds

Fill-in-the-blanks are a blast, but here are some ideas for creating some other word-game handouts using the One-With-Nature Hike scripture from this chapter.

Match, Natch!

Before photocopying, jot down the answer words in random order onto margins of the Biblical Fill-in-the-Blanks handouts (on preceding pages). Kids draw lines to match the words to the correct scripture. An impromptu game of "Mad Libs" might hatch from this match game!

Scramblin' Plan

Fill in all the blanks with the correct answers for the kids...but scramble up the letters of the words! Make photocopies of the handouts, and then challenge kids to unscramble for the correct words.

Cross Word

Use the scripture words to create a classic crossword puzzle or word-search game. It's easy to find free grids online for making your own word puzzles.

Craft Fun! Nature's Hang-up

Make fun, unique hanging mobiles with some of the stuff snagged during the hike. Handmade prayer beads (see Chapter 10: Love Thy Neighbor) make great spacers for mobiles.

DebHallPhotos21 /iStock/Thinkstock

What you need: branches and sticks, natural decor (shells, feathers, leaves, etc.), fishing line or any string, thin-gauge wire, scissors, hole punch, large sewing needle

1) Use sewing needle to string leaves and other items that are penetrable; rock-solid items can be wire-wrapped. Build your mobile from bottom to top, so begin with whatever you want dangling at the very end.

2) Tie that item to a stick, leaving enough line so the item hangs, then tie that stick to another, again leaving desired length of slack. Experiment with different constructions by tying items to the center of a stick or at its ends as you choose.

3) Repeat the process for as many tiers as you want in your mobile, moving the strings along each stick to find the balance points, until you've worked your way up to a solid base, which could be a sturdy piece of wood or several branches pieced together with string or wire.

4) Tie one last piece of string to the top, either centered or anchored at opposite ends of your top base, and the mobile is ready to hang out.

Log in Some Extra Fun

Want to gather up logs for the campfire and have fun at the same time? This quick scavenger hunt provides a sneaky way to send players on the prowl for firewood.

First look up the following scripture references, and write or print each verse in its entirety on a separate scrap of paper:

- Leviticus 14:10
- Leviticus 14:15
- Leviticus 14:21
- Leviticus 14:24
- 2 Samuel 5:11
- 1 Kings 5:8
- 1 Kings 5:10
- 1 Chronicles 14:1
- 1 Chronicles 22:4
- 2 Chronicles 2:3
- 2 Chronicles 2:8
- 2 Chronicles 2:16
- Ezra 3:7
- Ecclesiastes 10:9

Highlight the word *log* (or *logs*) in each of the printed scripture verses, then fold up the papers and toss them all into a hat or bowl. Pair up players, and have each duo pull a clue from the pile. Tell them to bring back whatever item corresponds with the highlighted word, and that they are to keep their clues secret from other players. Send them all off on the search, making sure there's access to wood piles if there isn't enough dry dead wood in the vicinity. By the time each team comes back, you'll have lots of logs for the fire—plus the kids will be all fired up because they'll now know they've just been pranked!

Need kindling, too? Print the following scripture on a piece of paper, highlight the word *kindling*, and toss it into the pile of clues.

As charcoal to embers and as wood to fire,
so is a quarrelsome person for kindling strife.

Proverbs 26:21

Stockbyte/Thinkstock

lilly3/iStock/Thinkstock

Whoever quarries stones may be injured by them;
whoever splits logs may be endangered by them.

Ecclesiastes 10:9

A Cut Above

Most national and state forests allow people to harvest trees for personal-use firewood, but safety is of the utmost importance, and you might need a permit. Contact the forest district office nearest you to obtain a firewood permit and tree-cutting instructions. Whether you're on private or public land, always have a skilled adult present when cutting firewood, and stick to these general guidelines from the United States Forest Service:

- *Tell someone where you are going and when you'll return.* Remember that cell phones might not get reception in many forests.
- *Know how to read a map and use a compass,* and carry them both with you.
- *Bring supplies*—including water, food, and a first-aid kit—to have in the event of an emergency.
- *Check weather conditions* and choose proper attire in the forests. Dress for the season.
- *Cut only dead trees* (without green) or down (windthrown) trees.

- *Check for trunk holes* and visible nests before cutting, since some dead trees provide animal habitats.
- *Keep stumps no higher than a foot* above the ground, preferably less.
- *Do not dump branches* or tops in roadside ditches or forest rights-of-way. Woody debris in ditches slows drainage and can cause erosion.
- *Leave all tops and branches* at least 25 feet into the woods. Roadside debris is a greater fire hazard.
- *Stay away from wet areas* alongside streams, rivers, and lakes. Check with a ranger for the proper distance to maintain.
- *Be aware* of areas where trees might be weakened by storms, insect damage, or fire.
- *Please clean up* after yourself.

The ax is already at the root of the trees, and every tree that does not produce good fruit will be cut down and thrown into the fire.

Matthew 3:10

Kesu01/Thinkstock

Pick up the Place

No need to take a hike for an excuse to clean up litter in surrounding areas. Plan a community cleanup day, encouraging kids to pick up trash in public places around the area…just because.

Fuse/Thinkstock

CHAPTER 2
Name Guessing Game

A good name is more desirable than great riches; to be esteemed is better than silver or gold.

Proverbs 22:1

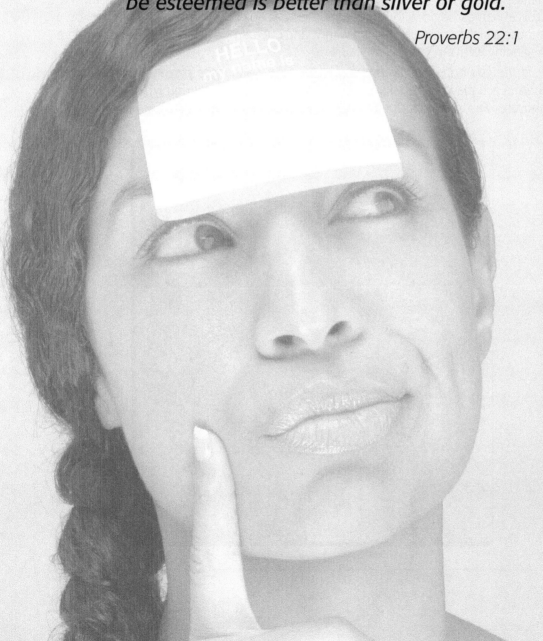

Name Guessing Game

This fun game uses biblical nametags, along with players' real names, as a get-acquainted activity—great for the first day of camp or a new youth group session! An alternate-twist version is provided for groups who already know one another's names. And, of course, the game can be tweaked to accommodate all-girls or -boys groups.

- *Make two lists of biblical names*, one male and the other female. Cut and paste names from online sources, or copy a list from a Bible index or reference book. Players will take on assigned biblical names that begin with the first and second letters of their real names, so be mindful of this when making the lists (see game rules in this chapter).

- *Choose names that are alphabetically closest* to the real names of players who are participating in the game, as there are literally hundreds of names in the Bible. No biblical names begin with W or X, by the way, so a player named William should choose a biblical name beginning with V, and one named Xavier should seek a name beginning with Y.

- *Post the lists on a bulletin board,* or tape to a wall where players can easily read them. Each player is to take on two biblical names, not randomly but deliberately chosen, which serve as clues for others to guess the player's real name.

Intellistudies/iStock/Thinkstock

What's Your Tag?

- *Pass out index cards or construction paper,* hole-punched so players can string yarn through them for hanging around their necks.
- *Players write their real names on the backs* of the cards, privately so others can't see. On the fronts of the nametags, players each write two assigned biblical names (one male and one female).
- *Call the girls first to the list* of female names, and then the boys to the male list, and instruct them to find a biblical name that begins with the first letter of their real name and write it on the front of the nametag (leave room to write below it). If there are a lot of players, call them in alphabetized groups—"Players whose names begin with the letter A may now approach the bulletin board."
- *Now have boys and girls switch spots* at the bulletin board. Girls go to the list of male biblical names, and boys look at the female names. Each player chooses a biblical name of the opposite sex that begins with the second letter of his or her actual name.

For example, a player whose real name is Heather writes *Heather* on the back of her tag, and on the front maybe *Hephzibah* near the top and *Elijah* below it. So other players know her real name begins with *HE—* but need to guess the rest.

Oleksii Nazarenko/iStock/Thinkstock

Name Game On!

- *Now, have players wear their nametags* so their biblical names are facing out for others to see but real names are not visible to other players.
- *Next, turn on some fun music*—maybe Bridgit Mendler's album *My Name Is…* It's time to mingle!
- *Players try to guess one another's names* with the biblical names providing clues as to the first two letters.
- *Someone correctly guesses a player's name?* The player who was named turns his tag around.
- *The game continues* until most or all players' tags reveal their real names.
- *Keep the mingling going* throughout the length of the music album—not too loud, for easy chatting—even if all the kids' names have been guessed so they can continue to get familiar with one another.

monkeybusinessimages/iStock/Thinkstock

Name Guessing Game Rules

- *Duplicate names are allowed*—if two girls named Heather are in the game, both can be name-tagged Hephzibah Elijah. This will help drive the game since both players, upon seeing each other's tag, might immediately guess that they share a name. Or maybe not. Perhaps she's Heidi—who knows?

- *Need to make it a little bit easier?* Tell players to draw dashes coinciding with the letters of their names at the very bottom of the front of their tags and fill in the two clues. So the bottom of Heather's tag is H E _ _ _ _ _, while Heidi's reads H E _ _ _.

- *Players whose actual names match up* to a biblical name may take on that same name. So a player named Mary might write *Mary* on both the back and front of her nametag, and perhaps *Abraham* below it on the front and then M A _ _. It'll be funny as kids forget to ask the obvious: "Is Mary your real name?"

- *Already know one another's names?* Do the tags in reverse. Write players' real names on the fronts and biblical names on the backs, and challenge them to guess the names from the Bible. For this version, you might choose more common biblical names, unless you want to stump players—then by all means, go with lesser-known Bible characters.

Craft Fun! Name Plates

While the kids are getting friendly, break out some art supplies—markers, watercolors, crayons, glitter, sequins, glue—and turn plain white paper plates into wall decor. On the back of his plate, each player is to write two lines of scripture that contain his assigned biblical names. Have players decorate the fronts with their real names in big letters. These plates will hang easily with masking tape above bunks or on lockers to help kids remember the names of their newfound friends.

vavit/iStock/Thinkstock

Munchie Madness

What? Paper plates with no food? Wouldn't hear of it! While the kids work on their art projects, leave out extra paper plates so they can pile on some snacks—following are fun party-mix ideas. Add equal parts of each ingredient, gauging amounts according to the number of hungry kids. For each recipe, simply toss all into a large bowl, mix up gently with a wooden spoon, and dig in. If you want, you can set out all the ingredients and let the kids do the mixing. Of course, feel free to make substitutions and add-ins. When it comes to a good party mix, anything goes!

wildpixel/iStock/Thinkstock

 **Recipe**

Fire-Hot Stuff

This snack mix doesn't burn like the devil—it isn't spicy or scorching, swear! But drop a handful onto a plate, and it resembles a blazing campfire.

Salted pretzel logs
Crunchy cheese-flavored snacks
Bite-size cheese crackers
Nacho-flavored tortilla chips
Sweet-potato chips, lightly broken

The Bible Adventure Book of Scavenger Hunts

 Recipe

Power Camo Ammo

Energize fatigued kids with this arsenal of yumminess that uses sweet and savory snack foods in neutral shades to create a camouflage effect. (Please omit the wasabi if serving to very young children.)

Sesame sticks
Wasabi peas
Banana chips
Coconut flakes
Cashew pieces

The Bible Adventure Book of Scavenger Hunts

 Recipe

Happy Trail Mix

For this recipe kids are challenged to look up each scripture reference to complete the ingredients, finding the food item that best fits from each verse cited. (Check out Chapter 4: Search for Your Supper for more recipes like this.)

Puffed whole-**Acts 27:38** cereal
Peanuts or any other **Song of Songs 6:11**
Jumbo or golden **1 Chronicles 16:3**
Sunflower or pumpkin **Leviticus 11:37**
Popped corn **Deuteronomy 23:25**

The Bible Adventure Book of Scavenger Hunts

Answer Key: Happy Trail Mix

- When they had eaten as much as they wanted, they lightened the ship by throwing the **grain** into the sea. Acts 27:38
- I went down to the grove of **nut** trees to look at the new growth in the valley, to see if the vines had budded or the pomegranates were in bloom. Song of Songs 6:11
- Then he gave a loaf of bread, a cake of dates and a cake of **raisins** to each Israelite man and woman. 1 Chronicles 16:3
- If a carcass falls on any **seeds** that are to be planted, they remain clean. Leviticus 11:37
- If you enter your neighbor's grainfield, you may pick **kernels** with your hands, but you must not put a sickle to their standing grain. Deuteronomy 23:25

Burst o' Thirst Quenchers

Set out three or four ice-packed coolers, each filled with one type of the following canned beverages. Label the outside of each cooler, replacing a keyword in the drink name with a scripture reference as listed here. Inside the cooler lids, tape the scripture with the correct fill-in-the-blank word highlighted. See if kids can guess what's in the coolers *before* opening the lids.

Root Beer
Frosty-top *Proverbs 12:12* Beer
The **root** of the righteous endures. Proverbs 12:12

Grape Soda
Sweet *Obadiah 1:5* Soda-pop
If **grape** pickers came to you, would they not leave a few grapes? Obadiah 1:5

Decaffeinated Cola
Cool Caffeine-*Galatians 5:1* Cola
It is for freedom that Christ has set us **free**. Galatians 5:1

Organic Green Tea
God's Good *Joel 2:22* Tea
The pastures in the wilderness are becoming **green**. Joel 2:22

CHAPTER 3
Garden of Seedin'

*Now the Lord God had planted a garden in the east,
in Eden; and there he put the man he had formed.*

Genesis 2:8

Garden of Seedin'

Based on gardening parables, this scavenger hunt incorporates scripture—and several strategically, um, well-planted seeds—to cultivate kids' growth in and through Christ's word. The game leads up to fun organic growing projects, with players collecting plant-seed of edibles found in the Bible. Before the hunt, read through all of the instructions first since you'll have to pre-pave some trails (using seed, nut, and fruit) and also plant clues in cleverly placed spots. Don't set it up too far in advance, since critters will surely snack on your trail if left out for long. Ground rules for players are provided in the handout on the opposite page.

kazoka30/iStock/Thinkstock

The promises were spoken to Abraham and to his seed.
Scripture does not say "and to seeds," meaning many people,
but "and to your seed," meaning one person, who is Christ.

Galatians 3:16

The Bible Adventure Book of Scavenger Hunts

Garden of Seedin' Ground Rules

- *Go in small groups,* collecting seeds, nuts, and fruits as you go along since you will need these for gardening projects at the end of the game.

- *It's fine to mix seeds* while gathering since they can be separated out later.

- *Bring along toting supplies, such as backpacks and containers.* Baby food jars (see Jarheads project in Chapter 1) make great little nut-and-seed containers.

- *Toss water bottles* into backpacks for thirst quenching.

- *Clues should be left wherever they're found,* so read each one to get directions to the next spot and then return the written clue to its original placement before moving on.

- *Gather only as much as you need,* generally just a few nuts or seeds and one piece of any fruit.

- *Sharing is encouraged!*

> **Abundance Abounds!**
>
> To demonstrate the nature of God's abundance, set up this scavenger-hunt route for more than one group on any given day. Forge the trail, letting younger players go first and then older kids later as the seeds diminish to make the game more challenging. Replenish exceptionally scant areas where needed before sending a new group on the never-ending search for good seed.

Paving the Pathway

Set up the trail of clues before the hunt. Photocopy the parable-themed clues, outlined in the following sections, and place in selected spots for the scavenger hunt.

Parable #1

The game can start from any location you choose. First, post the following clue (all scripture quotes are italicized) in plain sight in a spot—perhaps tacked to a bulletin board—where players can easily read it at the game's starting point.

The Sower and the Seeds

Matthew 13:3–9; Mark 4:3–9; Luke 8:5–8

Listen! A farmer went out to sow his seed.
Some fell on the path and became birdfeed.
Others wound up rocked and shocked,
Weathered and withered,
Drenched and quenched,
Scorched and torched,
Poked and choked,
Dried and fried.

Still other seed fell on good soil.
It shot up without getting spoiled.
With that in mind, take the almond-strewn trail
Until you arrive at the next Bible tale.

Parable #2

Drop a trail of raw shelled *almonds* for players to follow, leading to the next clue, which can be folded up and hidden (perhaps under a rock) or posted where players can easily spot it, depending on age and skill level.

The Grain of Wheat

John 12:23–26

The wonderful Christ Jesus once replied,
"The hour has come for the Son of Man to be glorified."
He went on to explain the wheat kernel that died.

"Whoever serves me must follow me;
And where I am, my servant also will be.
My father will honor the one who serves me."

The message is clear that He does reign
Since He certainly did not die in vain.
Now, follow the train of barley grain.

Parable #3

Leave a trail of *barley*, which leads to a grassy area where players will find more barley, as well as *lentil*, along with this clue, maybe buried under a handful of grass.

The Weeds in the Grain

Matthew 13:24–30

The kingdom of heaven
Is like a man who sowed good seed,
But while he was sleeping,
His enemy came and sowed weeds.

"Leave those weeds alone," He said,
"And let the good prevail instead."
Make like Jesus, and be very gentle,
As you pick up bits of barley and lentil.
Once you've collected a decent batch,
Follow the trail out of the grassy patch.

Parable #4

Put piles of barley and lentil in the grassy area so it has to be picked up among the grassy "weeds," then make a trail of lentil leading to an appropriate spot to plant the next clue.

The Seed Growing Secretly

Mark 4:26–29

This is what the kingdom of God is like.
A man scatters seed on the ground.
Night and day, whether he sleeps or gets up,
The seed sprouts and grows, though he does not know how.

God is good; God is just.
We thank Him for this coriander seed.
All we know is that we must trust,
And He will give us all we need.

Parable #5

From this spot, forge a trail of whole *coriander* seed for players to follow to this clue, also buried or hidden anyplace that's convenient or challenging.

The Mustard Seed

Matthew 13:31–32, Mark 4:30–32, Luke 13:18

The kingdom of heaven is like a mustard seed,
Which a man took and planted in his field.
Though it is the smallest of all seeds,
It creates a phenomenally large yield.

The seed in this hunt is getting smaller and smaller
For plants that potentially grow taller and taller.
So follow the mini mustard seed (see?)
Until you arrive at a fairly large tree.

Parable #6

Make a trail of *mustard* seed that leads to a tree, underneath which, to its left, you'll set a bowl of *olives* (with pits) serving as a paperweight for this clue.

The Two Olive Trees

Zechariah 4:1–14

The angel asked, "What do you see?"
There are two olive trees,
One on the right of the bowl
And the other on its left.

"Do you not know what these are?"
These are the two who are anointed
To serve the Lord of all the earth,
These two trees on the right and the left.

"Do you not know what these are?"
Beginning to feel like you've been strung along?
The olives are left of the nearest tree
So the next clue must be…right? Wrong!

aaron007/iStock/Thinkstock

Parable #7

Do not drop a trail of seeds at this point but instead, to the left of the bowl of olives, choose another tree from which you'll hang these three things: a string of *garlic* bulbs, an unopened package of *dates* (with pits), and an envelope holding this clue.

The Barren Fig Tree

Luke 13:6–9

A man had a fig tree,
But it was fruitless.
"Cut it down!
It's totally useless."

The gardener heard him,
For he was near:
"Leave it alone
For one more year."

Now here you are
By a tree so big.
And this one, too,
Hasn't a single fig.

It did grow garlic
It appears, as of late.
(Please don't eat it,
If you have a date.)

You will find some figs
And also grapes, please,
But no clear directions—
Look under more trees!

Parable #8

Again, do not drop a trail of seeds, but leave a box or basket, filled with fresh *figs* and seeded *grapes*, underneath another nearby tree. Inside the basket of fruit, tuck this clue.

The Tree and Its Fruit

Matthew 7:15–20, Luke 6:43–49

No good tree bears bad fruit,
Nor does a bad tree bear good fruit.
Each tree is recognized by its own fruit.

Is this false, or is it true?
Grapes are purple, and figs are too.
Roses are red, and violets are blue.
Rows of apples lead to your next clue.

Fuse/Thinkstock

Parable #9

From the produce box, which is filled with figs and grapes, begin a trail of well-spaced *apples* along the ground, guiding players to a basket of *cucumbers* with the next clue.

The Weather Signs

Luke 12:54–56

You say, "It's going to rain."
You say, "It's going to be hot."
You act as cool as a cucumber,
Even when you're not!

When you see a cloud rising in the west,
And when the south wind blows,
That's the direction you'll find is best
When it's time to go with the flow.

And how exactly will you know?
South, west, which way to go?

You know how to interpret
The appearance of the earth and sky.
How is it that you don't know how
To interpret this present time?

Wake up, peeps! It's time for jellin'
Over God's juiciest, sweetest seasonal melon!

ChiccoDodiFC/Shutterstock.com

Parable #10

The previous clue requires players to use directional skills, so leave the last bounty (*melons*) at a place located southwest from that point, with the last clue tucked in with a group of watermelon, cantaloupe, honeydew, or any other melon varieties.

The Flowers of the Field

Matthew 6:28–34, Luke 12:27–31

In a hurry? Do not worry.
See how the flowers of the field grow.
They do not labor or spin.

"What shall we eat?"
"What shall we drink?"
Duh! God always provides.
What do ya think?

There's always abundance;
God knows all your needs.
He always gives plenty,
When you plant the seeds.

God said, "I give you every seed-bearing plant on
the face of the whole earth and every tree that has fruit
with seed in it. They will be yours for food."

Genesis 1:29

tchara/iStock/Thinkstock

Root-and-Shoot Experiment

From the Bible-based seed-bearing foods collected in the hunt (noted in the following list), experiment with planting different seeds in various ways so kids can attempt to grow full-on plants from seed. In some cases, that will mean eating fruits to get to the seeds—yum! (Check out the Need a Reason for the Seedin'? section in this chapter.)

Anything that successively sprouts can be planted in a community garden. Of course, feel free to experiment also with other common summer food fare, such as tomato, lemon, or sunflower seeds. Some dry seeds can be bought inexpensively and in large quantities. Coriander, for example, is not necessarily easy to seed from fresh cilantro—but whole coriander seed is available in the spice aisle of many grocery stores. What follows is a list of all the foods used for the scavenger hunt. Use it as a shopping checklist, and, of course, try to buy organic:

- ❏ Almonds (raw shelled)
- ❏ Apples (any variety)
- ❏ Barley (pearl or hulled)
- ❏ Coriander (whole seed)
- ❏ Cucumbers (whole fresh)
- ❏ Dates (packaged organic)
- ❏ Figs (fresh, raw)
- ❏ Garlic (whole bulbs)
- ❏ Grapes (any with seeds)
- ❏ Lentils (dried packaged)
- ❏ Melons (seasonal varieties)
- ❏ Mustard (whole seed)
- ❏ Olives (cured with pits)

That's the Pits!

Be mindful of what you're buying. For this hunt, do not buy seedless grapes or olives, for example. Opposite of what you might think, the words "pitted" and "seeded" on food packaging sometimes mean pits and seeds have been removed (but not always, so pay attention). Likewise, "shelled" nuts aren't always in their shells. For the purpose of this scavenger hunt, always go for the stuff with seeds.

Science Project: Yes, You Can

Since this is a science-based project in which players test different ways of germinating seeds, provided are just some general guidelines and quick tips to, well, get growing.

LeventKonuk/iStock/Thinkstock

What you need: empty clean tin cans, small rocks or gravel, potting soil, various seeds, Popsicle sticks, permanent markers, water, sunshine

1) *Collect seeds from hunt* or from recipes in Chapter 4 (for example, slice or core cucumbers and apples, and plant seeds or stash in paper towels for later).

2) *Gather tin cans* and any other small containers that can be reused for starting seeds. Egg cartons are great for planting dozens of small seedlings.

3) *Place a small handful of rocks* or gravel at bottoms of tins, for drainage, before adding soil.

4) *Clean seeds under running water* first to remove any pulp. Some require drying out, while others need to be soaked overnight (see guidelines that follow).

5) *Have kids choose seeds* they want to place in soil-filled tin cans, pushing seeds gently about a half-inch down and then covering with the soil.

6) *Use markers to write on Popsicle sticks* the names of the seeds and the person who planted them, and then insert those into the tins accordingly.

7) *Place tins in a sunny area,* and give them water daily. If kids want to take their plants home for continued care, cover the tops of tins with plastic wrap and secure with rubber bands.

Growing Pains and Gains

Monitor the progress of plant shoots by keeping a chart or individual journals, logging watering times, weather conditions, and planting methods. Transplant into the ground or in larger containers as the plants' growth warrants. Designate a plot of ground for outdoor gardening, allowing kids to help cultivate a garden throughout the growing season. Always give plants plenty of love—even before they've sprouted!

fotokostic/iStock/Thinkstock

Root-and-Shoot Growth Guidelines

Almond

- Use a nutcracker to remove almonds from shells.
- Put raw almonds in water and leave in a cool place.
- Plant when they have sprouts on ends.

Apple

- Soak seeds overnight in warm water.
- Plant a half dozen or more seeds.
- Seeds can take weeks to germinate.

Barley

- Barley prefers colder weather conditions.
- Grow large quantities in rows.
- Wear sleeves when harvesting (ouch!).

Coriander

- Look for bags of whole seeds at ethnic markets.
- Plant several seeds 1/4-inch deep.
- Seeds take three to four weeks to germinate.

Cucumber

- Dry seeds before planting.
- Plant four to five seeds.
- Let grow three inches before replanting.

stevehullphotography/iStock/Thinkstock

Date

- Most grocers sell packaged dates.
- Eat the dates, and save the seeds.
- Soak seeds for 48 hours before planting.

Fig

- Clean fruit's flesh from seeds.
- Allow seeds to dry out for two days.
- Place plastic wrap over tin for humidity.

Garlic

- Separate cloves from a fresh garlic bulb.
- Each clove is a potential plant.
- Push two inches into the soil, tips pointed upward.

Fuse/Thinkstock

Grape

- Spit out and save pits from grapes.
- Soak the seeds overnight.
- Throw away any seeds that float.

Fuse/Thinkstock

Lentil

- Dried lentils are available in grocery stores.
- Plant about a half dozen of the lentils.
- Expect three to four months for the plants to mature.

Melon

- Soak the seeds for two days before planting.
- Plant two seeds of each variety per tin.
- Weed out the weaker of the two when sprouted.

Mustard

- Get mustard seed from the grocer's spice aisle.
- Plant as is, no soaking or drying required.
- Produces edible greens and also seed for fresh mustard.

Olive

- Remove as much flesh as you can from the pits.
- Soak pits overnight in lukewarm water.
- Seeds that float are rotten, so toss those out.

cookie_cutter/iStock/Thinkstock

Need a Reason for the Seedin'?

Whether you're gardening or not, here are a few fun excuses for getting to the core of God's good fruit.

Diet Cuke

Sliced cucumber tastes surprisingly delicious in iced water, adding extra vitamins and minerals. Also consider tossing fresh mint into the water. Put this same water in a squirt bottle (or water pistol!) for a refreshing body spritzer.

Sparkle Grapes

Remove grapes from stems, and place them, cleaned and completely dried, inside ice cube trays and then fill with sparkling water. Place in freezer for several hours, and then use as cubes to chill a drink or just enjoy as a frozen snack—*brrr*.

Watermelon Slush

Fill a blender with seedless watermelon chunks, a handful of ice, a few loose mint leaves, a squeeze of lime, and a drop of honey, and blend until smooth. Serve with straws, and sip up!

utah778/iStock/Thinkstock

Not for Green Thumbs Only

If you prefer a less complex gardening activity, or on the flip side want to round out your already elaborate community garden, go for any of these easy-peasy projects.

Pot o' Beans

Simply pick up an inexpensive bag of assorted dried beans from the grocery store's soup aisle. Germinate one week before planting by folding inside moist paper towels and placing in plastic baggies until sprouts appear.

Spice It Up!

While you're in the spice cabinet pulling down the mustard seed, what else can you try planting? Cumin and dill commonly come in seed form, and both are specifically referred to in the Bible. Try also anise, caraway, celery, fennel, or sesame seed.

Lily Rose

Numerous references to lilies and roses are scattered throughout scriptures. Lilies are grown from bulbs, roses from seed or cuttings. Since there are loads of easy-to-grow varieties, do some research before choosing.

I am a rose of Sharon, a lily of the valleys.

Song of Songs 2:1

Rodrigo_Albertini/iStock/Thinkstock

How Does Your Garden Grow?

Following are a few final tips for putting the *fun* in functional when it comes to cultivating a church or community garden.

moodboard

Good Wood

Wooden pallets, mounted to the side of a building or fence, make fab shelving for gardening supplies and potted shoots. An adult who's sufficiently skilled in carpentry can remove slats from the fronts to make shelf bottoms. Let kids have fun painting pallets before hanging.

Community Compost

To have rich gardening soil readily available from one season to the next, create a compost pile—be sure it's covered and stored where wild critters can't get to it. Food scraps such as eggshells, fruit rinds, and cornhusks, as well as garden clippings and paper trash, can be composted. Many online sources have details about how to build and maintain a compost bin, so get cracking.

Decor Galore

Feel inspired to further spiff up the garden? Paint tin cans before using as planters. Adorn the garden area with colorful fabric scraps, jump ropes, and stringed pop-top rings. Give worn lawn furniture a shot of metallic spray paint. Use stones and marbles to make mosaics in the ground. Stretch the decoration imagination!

*The garden had hangings of white and blue linen,
fastened with cords of white linen and purple material to
silver rings on marble pillars. There were couches of gold
and silver on a mosaic pavement of porphyry, marble,
mother-of-pearl and other costly stones.*

Esther 1:6

archideaohoto/iStock/Thinkstock

CHAPTER 4
Search for Your Supper

I saw an angel standing in the sun, who cried in a loud voice to all the birds flying in midair, "Come, gather together for the great supper of God."

Revelation 19:17

Search for Your Supper

This scavenger hunt provides recipes that use only foods found in the Bible. Kids must scour the campground or recreational area to find the correct ingredients for each dinner course. The game ends with a cookout, in which players get to flex their culinary skills.

God's Dinner Menu

Each recipe is for one serving—photocopy, cut, and hand out so every player has his own complete set of recipe cards. Kids collect all the ingredients they need for their dinner, but must first look up the scriptures referenced to find the keywords to complete the correct food items (a full grocery list is provided at the end of this chapter).

Tell players to find the food-based word in each verse that best completes its ingredient, and then send them off to gather groceries. Once they've collected all of the food, the kids then assemble and prepare their own meals with adult supervision to oversee cutting and cooking procedures.

Recipe

Garden-of-Eden Salad

This chopped salad has some unexpected ingredients, but the fresh flavors combine well, along with a tangy dressing.

1 baby **Jeremiah 10:5**
1 hardboiled **Luke 11:12**
5 seedless **Deuteronomy 24:20**

2 fresh **Luke 11:42** leaves
1/2 teaspoon canola **Matthew 6:17**
1/4 teaspoon white **Psalm 69:21**

Carefully chop the first four ingredients and place in a small bowl. Add the remaining, and toss lightly to mix until coated with dressing.

The Bible Adventure Book of Scavenger Hunts

DebHallPhotos21/iStock/Thinkstock

Answer Key: Garden-of-Eden Salad

- Like a scarecrow in a **cucumber** field, their idols cannot speak. Jeremiah 10:5
- Or if he asks for an **egg**, will give him a scorpion? Luke 11:12
- When you beat the **olives** from your trees, do not go over the branches a second time. Deuteronomy 24:20
- You give God a tenth of your **mint**, rue and all other kinds of garden herbs. Luke 11:42
- But when you fast, put **oil** on your head and wash your face. Matthew 6:17
- They put gall in my food and gave me **vinegar** for my thirst. Psalm 69:21

Recipe

Hot-Mess Mini-Loaf

No need to pre-thaw the frozen patties since a warm climate (and working hands) take care of that quickly.

1 4-oz. frozen ground **Exodus 22:31** patty, thawed

1 slice **John 6:35**, torn into pieces

1 tablespoon **Hebrews 5:13**

1 single-serve packet **Matthew 17:20** or ketchup

1 slice of **1 Samuel 17:18**, torn into pieces

1 sprig fresh **Numbers 11:7**, chopped

Mix all of the ingredients, in the order listed, in a small bowl, working with hands until well combined. Shape into a small oval. Tightly double-wrap in two sheets of aluminum foil (to tell loaves apart, first personalize by using permanent marker to write initials on outside of foil). Grill over an open flame, turning over once, or bake in oven on a cookie sheet at 350 degrees, for 30 minutes until cooked through. Let sit a few minutes before unwrapping.

The Bible Adventure Book of Scavenger Hunts

David De Lossy/Photodisc/Thinkstock

Answer Key: Hot-Mess Mini-Loaf

- You are to be my holy people. So do not eat the **meat** of an animal torn by wild beasts; throw it to the dogs. Exodus 22:31
- Then Jesus declared, "I am the **bread** of life. Whoever comes to me will never go hungry, and whoever believes in me will never be thirsty." John 6:35
- Anyone who lives on **milk**, being still an infant, is not acquainted with the teaching about righteousness. Hebrews 5:13
- He replied, "Because you have so little faith. Truly I tell you, if you have faith as small as a **mustard** seed, you can say to this mountain, 'Move from here to there,' and it will move. Nothing will be impossible for you." Matthew 17:20
- Take along these ten **cheeses** to the commander of their unit. See how your brothers are and bring back some assurance from them. 1 Samuel 17:18
- The manna was like **coriander** seed and looked like resin. Numbers 11:7

Recipe

Moral-Fiber Fun Dish

This one-pot side dish is packed with deliciousness...and "nutritiousness."

1 cup spring or tap **John 4:14**
1 **Deuteronomy 11:10** bouillon cube
1/4 cup dried red **2 Samuel 23:11**
1 tablespoon pearled **Ruth 2:17**

1 tablespoon slivered **Numbers 17:8**
1 pat of **Psalm 55:21**
A dash of **Luke 14:34**

Have each dinner guest toss all ingredients together into one large pot (or several, if you have a large group). Bring to boil over an open flame or on stovetop. Cover, and let simmer half an hour until legumes and grains are tender. Continue to cook, uncovered, a few minutes to reduce liquid if necessary.

The Bible Adventure Book of Scavenger Hunts

LiciaR/iStock/Thinkstock

Answer Key: Moral-Fiber Fun Dish

- But whoever drinks the **water** I give them will never thirst. Indeed, the water I give them will become in them a spring of water welling up to eternal life. John 4:14
- The land you are entering to take over is not like the land of Egypt, from which you come, where you planted your seed and irrigated it by foot as in a **vegetable** garden. Deuteronomy 11:10
- When the Philistines banded together at a place where there was a field full of **lentils**, Israel's troops fled from them. 2 Samuel 23:11
- So Ruth gleaned in the field until evening. Then she threshed the **barley** she had gathered, and it amounted to about an ephah. Ruth 2:17
- The next day Moses entered the tent and saw that Aaron's staff, which represented the tribe of Levi, had not only sprouted but had budded, blossomed and produced **almonds**. Numbers 17:8
- His talk is smooth as **butter**, yet war is in his heart; his words are more soothing than oil, yet they are drawn swords. Psalm 55:21
- **Salt** is good. But if it loses its saltiness, how can it be made salty again? Luke 14:34

Recipe

Nothin' Fancy Fruit Tartlet

This fun fresh-fruit dessert is cooked in classic canning jar lids, which serve as little "pie pans."

1/2 peeled **Psalm 17:8**, cored and sliced
1 teaspoon pure **Psalm 19:10**
1/2 teaspoon all-purpose **Isaiah 47:2**

1/4 teaspoon ground **Exodus 30:23**
1 tablespoon chilled pie **Romans 11:16**

Toss first four ingredients into a small bowl, and stir until well combined; set aside. Take a clean wide-mouth canning jar lid and ring, and turn the cap so its rubber part is facing the top of the lid and the metal part inside. Now use thumbs to press the last ingredient into the lid and up its sides. Spoon fruit filling into the crust, and wrap loosely but securely in foil. Bake on cookie sheets in 400-degree oven, or on indirect heat if cooking outdoors, for 20 to 25 minutes. Let cool, and then push the lid up through its ring to loosen the tart from the lid. Serve with a scoop of any flavor **Job 37:10** cream.

The Bible Adventure Book of Scavenger Hunts

erin_gleeson/iStock/Thinkstock

Answer Key: Nothin' Fancy Fruit Tartlet

- Keep me as the **apple** of your eye; hide me in the shadow of your wings. Psalm 17:8
- They are more precious than gold, than much pure gold; they are sweeter than **honey**, than honey from the honeycomb. Psalm 19:10
- Take millstones and grind **flour**; take off your veil. Lift up your skirts, bare your legs, and wade through the streams. Isaiah 47:2
- Take the following fine spices: 500 shekels of liquid myrrh, half as much (that is, 250 shekels) of fragrant **cinnamon**, 250 shekels of fragrant calamus. Exodus 30:23
- If the part of the **dough** offered as firstfruits is holy, then the whole batch is holy; if the root is holy, so are the branches. Romans 11:16.
- The breath of God produces **ice**, and the broad waters become frozen. Job 37:10

Extra! Extra! Snazz it Up!

Flex and stretch the kids' culinary creativity by challenging them to incorporate into their recipes any of these additional ingredients, also found in the Bible:

• Beans	• Garlic	• Olive oil
• Cumin	• Grapes	• Onion
• Dill	• Leeks	• Pistachios
• Dates	• Melon	• Raisins

Monkey Business Images/Thinkstock

Prep Rally!

TAGSTOCK1/iStock/Thinkstock

These are a few things to consider when planning this scavenger hunt:

- *Players need to have access to the kitchen* or pantry, and perhaps a vegetable garden, depending on where food items are located. If you want to make it extra challenging— for instance, hide the hardboiled eggs like an Easter hunt—go for it!

- *Hand out grocery bags for kids* to carry their finds. Each recipe is for one serving, so every player has to gather exactly enough food for her own supper.

- *Provide small plastic condiment cups with lids* or baby-food jars for collecting teaspoon amounts of ingredients such as oil or spices, and brown paper lunch bags for things like nuts and lentils. When possible, provide individual-size products, such as half-pint cartons of milk (kids can measure out when food-prepping and drink the rest).

- *Make sure there's access to measuring utensils* where needed. Also, tell players it's okay to mix ingredients while gathering, as long as they are within the same recipe; otherwise, contain separately.

- *Make scripture tags for each ingredient* to mark successful finds. For example, write Jeremiah 10:5 (see Garden-of-Eden Salad recipe) on an index card, and post it in the cucumber garden or on a basket of baby cukes so kids know when they've found a matching ingredient.

- *Be sure there's a clean prep area* for cutting veggies and doing other preparations, and use discretion as far as age appropriateness when it comes to cooking procedures. Have kids thoroughly wash their hands before handling food.

- *Remember to say a blessing* before eating.

Wavebreakmedia/ iStock/Thinkstock

*Blessed are those who hunger and thirst
for righteousness, for they will be filled.*

Matthew 5:6

Room for S'More?

Kids might be full—and tired. But they'll love you for sending them on their way with a little nibble for later. Set out three large bowls filled to the brim with graham-cracker bears, mini-marshmallows, and chocolate chips, then give each player a flat-bottomed ice-cream cone to fill with…mmm, s'more snacks.

John Lund/Sam Diephuis/Blend Images/Thinkstock

Grocery List

Time to stock up on groceries! A single unit is needed for each serving (for instance, you'll need one baby cucumber and an egg for each participant), so simply multiply by how many participants you have. For items that need to be measured or counted, such as oil and olives, check recipes to gauge the amounts you'll need.

Garden-of-Eden Salad

- ❏ Baby cucumbers
- ❏ Hardboiled eggs
- ❏ Seedless olives
- ❏ Fresh mint or other herbs
- ❏ Canola oil
- ❏ White vinegar

Hot-Mess Mini-Loaf

- ❏ Frozen ground meat patties
- ❏ Sliced whole-wheat bread
- ❏ Low-fat milk
- ❏ Mustard and ketchup packets
- ❏ Cheese slices
- ❏ Fresh coriander, or cilantro

Moral-Fiber Fun Dish

- ❏ Spring water
- ❏ Vegetable bouillon cubes
- ❏ Dried red lentils
- ❏ Slivered almonds
- ❏ Butter
- ❏ Salt

Nothin' Fancy Fruit Tartlet

- ❏ Apples
- ❏ Pure honey
- ❏ All-purpose flour
- ❏ Ground cinnamon
- ❏ Pie dough
- ❏ Ice cream, any flavor

Snazzy Extra Add-Ins

- ❏ Beans
- ❏ Cumin
- ❏ Dill
- ❏ Dates
- ❏ Garlic
- ❏ Grapes
- ❏ Leeks
- ❏ Melon
- ❏ Olive oil
- ❏ Onion
- ❏ Pistachios
- ❏ Raisins

S'more Snack Cones

- ❏ Graham-cracker bears
- ❏ Mini-marshmallows
- ❏ Chocolate chips
- ❏ Ice cream cones

Fuse/Thinkstock

Don't Trash It—Stash It!

Save certain "garbage" items from group meals to be used for art projects and other activities in this book. Have kids thoroughly rinse out and then toss the following in bins marked for "upcycling":

- Plastic containers or baby food jars (nature collecting, Chapter 3)
- Egg cartons (gardening, Chapter 3)
- Tin cans with lids removed (gardening, Chapter 3)
- Popsicle sticks (garden markers, Chapter 3; frames, Chapter 8)
- Canning jar lids (fruit tartlets, Chapter 4)
- Milk cartons (bird feeders, Chapter 6)
- Clear glass bottles (rainbow experiment, Chapter 7; treasure map, Chapter 11)
- Paper towel rolls (kaleidoscopes, Chapter 11)
- Cereal boxes (kaleidoscopes, Chapter 11)
- Flimsy plastic produce containers (kaleidoscopes, Chapter 11)
- Ice cream buckets (party supplies, Chapter 12)

Ryan McVay/DigitalVision/Thinkstock

CHAPTER 5
Lost and Found

*Ask and it will be given to you;
seek and you will find.*

Matthew 7:7

Lost and Found

This stealth version of a scavenger hunt plants a notebook in the lost-and-found box for the first unsuspecting kid who comes along. Clues, handwritten or pasted in the pages of the notebook, require kids to search their imaginations before circling back to the lost-and-found area, where the book is left for another player.

- *Buy a blank notebook,* something heavy-duty that will make a good scrapbook, and write *Finders Keepers!* on the cover, and then your group's name and the year underneath that. Add another tagline, such as *It's okay! Take a peek…* maybe with a sketch of a set of eyeballs, to encourage kids to open the book.
- *Deliberately leave the book in the lost-and-found box,* to be passed around in a continuous cycle, similar to a "poetry slam book," for kids to write, draw, tape, glitter, and glue, based on hints within the book, which always winds up back at the lost-and-found, and so on.
- *Copy or paste the scripture* and text, outlined in this chapter, into the notebook as hints to prompt kids' creativity. Also include the accompanying artwork, or use it as inspiration to include your own art inside the book's pages, whether drawing or collaging.
- *Leave many blank pages* between prompts for kids to express themselves, spacing each hint far apart. After first labeling the front of the notebook with *Finders Keepers!,* copy, cut, and paste this text on the inside cover:

Losers weepers?
Jeepers creepers!
Ah, yikes! Oh, dear!
What have we here?

Have no sorrow
You can borrow
Please, just bring it
Back tomorrow

Draw a minute
Write a vignette
You're feeling pinched?
It's packed with hints

Follow them all
You'll have a ball
Or do a few
It's up to you

Yes, you can share
That's, if you dare
To let someone
In on the fun!

On the very first page of the notebook, paste the following scripture-themed hint (and accompanying artwork, if desired) to serve as the first prompt to inspire kids to express themselves creatively. Leaf through several blank pages before copying and pasting the next hint, continuing until the book is filled with creative prompts. By all means, put your own artistic expression into this project as you build the book's contents!

Hint #1

The Book of the Law Found

When the king heard the words of the Book of the Law, he tore his robes. "Because your heart was responsive and you humbled yourself before the Lord when you heard what I have spoken—and because you tore your robes and wept in my presence, I also have heard you," declares the Lord.

2 Kings 22:11, 19

Staple, clip, or glue onto these pages, a small scrap of fabric that represents you—a bit of bandanna, denim cut-off threads, a hair ribbon. Sign your name next to it… unless you prefer to remain anonymous.

Stuart101276/iStock/Thinkstock

Hint #2

The Lost Sheep

Suppose one of you has a hundred sheep and loses one of them. Doesn't he leave the ninety-nine in the open country and go after the lost sheep until he finds it? And when he finds it, he joyfully puts it on his shoulders and goes home. Then he calls his friends and neighbors together and says, "Rejoice with me; I have found my lost sheep." I tell you that in the same way there will be more rejoicing in heaven over one sinner who repents than over ninety-nine righteous persons who do not need to repent.

Luke 15:1–7

Have you ever lost something really precious to you that you still haven't found? Sketch a picture of it.

MADandFORK/iStock/Thinkstock

*My people have been lost sheep; their shepherds
have led them astray and caused them to roam
on the mountains. They wandered over mountain
and hill and forgot their own resting place.*

Jeremiah 50:6

Hint #3

The Lost Coin

Suppose a woman has ten silver coins and loses one. Doesn't she light a lamp, sweep the house and search carefully until she finds it? And when she finds it, she calls her friends and neighbors together and says, "Rejoice with me; I have found my lost coin." In the same way, I tell you, there is rejoicing in the presence of the angels of God over one sinner who repents.

Luke 15:8–10

If you were to find something awesome that didn't belong to you, would you return it? Trace a coin here, and jot *yes* or *no* inside the circle. Then, around the traced coin, write one word, such as *compassion* or *confusion* that describes why you answered that way.

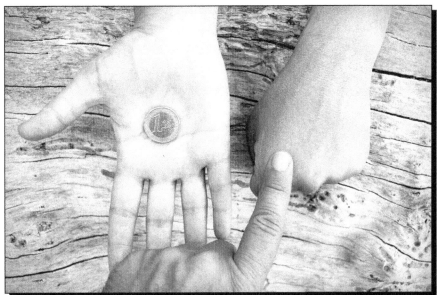

benjaminec/iStock/Thinkstock

Hint #4

The Lost Son

There was a man who had two sons. The younger son got together all he had, set off for a distant country and there squandered his wealth in wild living. "I will set out and go back to my father and say to him: Father, I have sinned against heaven and against you." His father saw him and was filled with compassion for him. The father said to his servants, "Quick! Bring the best robe and put it on him. Put a ring on his finger and sandals on his feet. For this son of mine was dead and is alive again; he was lost and is found."

Luke 15:11, 13, 18, 20, 22, 24

Have you ever lost and then found something that was important to you? Write, in one sentence, how that felt.

adelartworks/iStock/Thinkstock

Hint #5

The Stray Ox

If you see your fellow Israelite's ox or sheep straying, do not ignore it but be sure to take it back to its owner. If they do not live near you or if you do not know who owns it, take it home with you and keep it until they come looking for it. Then give it back. Do the same if you find their donkey or cloak or anything else they have lost.

Deuteronomy 22:1–3

Draw a picture or glue a photo of your favorite pet—real or imaginary—onto these pages.

Digital Vision/Photodisc/Thinkstock

As for the donkeys you lost three days ago,
do not worry about them; they have been found.

1 Samuel 9:20

Hint #6

The Ship That Sailed

Much time had been lost, and sailing had already become dangerous because by now it was after the Day of Atonement. So Paul warned them, "Men, I can see that our voyage is going to be disastrous and bring great loss to ship and cargo, and to our own lives also."

Acts 27:9–10

On a loose sheet of paper, write a short piece of prose about finding hope in what seemed like a missed opportunity. Fold it into an origami sailboat, and either keep it or tape it into this book.

Dynamic Graphics/Creatas/Thinkstock

Sail Away!

Copy and paste Classic Sailboat origami instructions (from Chapter 10) onto a page near Hint #6.

I urge you to keep up your courage, because not one of you will be lost; only the ship will be destroyed.

Acts 27:22

Hint #7

The Faded Precious Metal

How the gold has lost its luster, the fine gold become dull! The sacred gems are scattered at every street corner.

Lamentations 4:1

Tape or glue something (anything!) in here that's golden—a game token, metallic stickers, foil wrappers, sequins, glitter…

Jupiterimages/Thinkstock

Hint #8

The Completed Wall

I had rebuilt the wall and not a gap was left in it—though up to that time I had not set the doors in the gates. They were all trying to frighten us, thinking, "Their hands will get too weak for the work, and it will not be completed." But I prayed, "Now strengthen my hands." So the wall was completed…in fifty-two days. When all our enemies heard about this, all the surrounding nations were afraid and lost their self-confidence, because they realized that this work had been done with the help of our God.

Nehemiah 6:1, 9, 15–16

Leave your handprint here by tracing with a marker or dipping in finger paint. Then embellish your print with artwork or words that honestly express strength through God.

Wavebreakmedia Ltd/Thinkstock

Hint #9

The Bald Forehead

A man who has lost his hair and is bald is clean. If he has lost his hair from the front of his scalp and has a bald forehead, he is clean.

Leviticus 13:40–41

Get a piece of yarn, string, floss, or—do you dare?—gently pluck a single strand of hair from your own head, and glue it to this man's scalp!

Image Source Pink/Image Source/Thinkstock

But now we have lost our appetite;
we never see anything but this manna!

Numbers 11:6

Hint #10

The Budding Staff

The Lord said to Moses, "Put back Aaron's staff in front of the ark of the covenant law, to be kept as a sign to the rebellious. This will put an end to their grumbling against me, so that they will not die." Moses did just as the Lord commanded him. The Israelites said to Moses, "We will die! We are lost, we are all lost!"

Numbers 17:10–12

Ever conquer something everyone else said was a lost cause? Do tell!

MOF/iStock/Thinkstock

Hint #11

The Resurrection

And if Christ has not been raised, your faith is futile; you are still in your sins. Then those also who have fallen asleep in Christ are lost. If only for this life we have hope in Christ, we are of all people most to be pitied. But Christ has indeed been raised from the dead, the firstfruits of those who have fallen asleep.

1 Corinthians 15:16–20

Write a short bedtime prayer. Say it silently, or share it with a friend or bunkmates at lights-out. And come morning, wake up to Christ!

Jupiterimages/Creatas/Thinkstock

On the inside back cover of the notebook, leave a reminder to return the book to the lost-and-found:

You've had your turn
Now please return
To lost-and-found
For the next round

Of players who
Can have fun too
With this notebook—
The one you took!

So get on track
To take it back
And thanks so much
For the art and such…

MrIncredible/iStock/Thinkstock

*They must return what they have stolen
or taken by extortion, or what was entrusted
to them, or the lost property they found.*
Leviticus 6:4

CHAPTER 6
Raiders of Noah's Ark

*You are to bring into the ark two of all living creatures,
male and female, to keep them alive with you.*

Genesis 6:19

Raiders of Noah's Ark

This match game randomly couples players up into teams of two! Each duo works together to find a pair of the same animal. Since you probably don't live at a zoo and certainly don't want kids approaching live wildlife, players scour for matches in any form—plush teddy bear, monkey keychain, elephant earrings, rubber snake, bird on a sports-team cap, and so on.

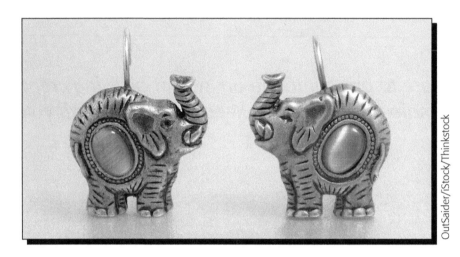

OutSaider/iStock/Thinkstock

- *Make two photocopies of the list of scripture clues* (see Into the Wild section on the opposite page), and cut them into separate strips. You'll need two of the same clue for every two players, so plan accordingly.
- *Fold the strips, and throw them into a bowl for a random drawing.* Or if you want, for instance, to have boy-girl teams (must be an even number of players), toss each list's strips into a separate bowl.
- *Have each player pull a strip from a bowl.* Tell him to read the scripture, and then find and pair up with the person who has the exact same clue.
- *Teams of two go on the prowl* for twins (not necessarily identical) of the animal highlighted on their scripture clue, collecting team-mascot attire, wilderness-themed magazines, stuffed animals, and such. Encourage teams to be cooperative rather than competitive, to help one another with difficult-to-find items.

Game Variation

Playing with a small group? Instead of paired teams, players go solo. Make only one copy of each scripture, but players are still expected to bring back two of each animal. These do not need to match exactly. For example, a player who has *dog* might bring a plush toy along with a family-pet photo. Each time a player comes back with a pair of critters, he gets to pull a new clue.

Ingram Publishing/Thinkstock

Into the Wild

Players search the grounds for the **bolded** creatures from the scriptures below and on the next page. If you need more clues, pull from the Birds of the Bible section in this chapter.

- Your children have fainted; they lie at every street corner, like **antelope** caught in a net. They are filled with the wrath of the Lord, with the rebuke of your God. Isaiah 51:20
- The king had a fleet of trading ships at sea along with the ships of Hiram. Once every three years it returned, carrying gold, silver and ivory, and **apes** and baboons. 1 Kings 10:22
- Better to meet a **bear** robbed of her cubs than a fool bent on folly. Proverbs 17:12
- In the Lord I take refuge. How then can you say to me: "Flee like a **bird** to your mountain." Psalm 11:1
- You blind guides! You strain out a gnat but swallow a **camel**. Matthew 23:24
- The Sovereign Lord is my strength; he makes my feet like the feet of a **deer**, he enables me to tread on the heights. Habakkuk 3:19
- Like one who grabs a stray **dog** by the ears is someone who rushes into a quarrel not their own. Proverbs 26:17
- Who let the wild **donkey** go free? Who untied its ropes? Job 39:5
- Speak to the earth, and it will teach you, or let the **fish** in the sea inform you. Job 12:8
- Catch for us the **foxes**, the little foxes that ruin the vineyards, our vineyards that are in bloom. Song of Songs 2:25
- Their land teemed with **frogs**, which went up into the bedrooms of their rulers. Psalm 105:30

- Make curtains of **goat** hair for the tent over the tabernacle—eleven altogether. Exodus 26:7
- Moreover, the Lord your God will send the **hornet** among them until even the survivors who hide from you have perished. Deuteronomy 7:20
- Do you give the **horse** its strength or clothe its neck with a flowing mane? Job 39:19
- **Hyenas** will inhabit her strongholds, jackals her luxurious palaces. Her time is at hand, and her days will not be prolonged. Isaiah 13:22
- Can an Ethiopian change his skin or a **leopard** its spots? Neither can you do good who are accustomed to doing evil. Jeremiah 13:23
- A nation has invaded my land, a mighty army without number; it has the teeth of a **lion**, the fangs of a lioness. Joel 1:6
- Do not muzzle an **ox** while it is treading out the grain. Deuteronomy 25:4
- Like a gold ring in a **pig**'s snout is a beautiful woman who shows no discretion. Proverbs 11:22
- The **rabbit**, though it chews the cud, does not have a divided hoof; it is unclean for you. Leviticus 11:6
- For you were like **sheep** going astray, but now you have returned to the Shepherd and Overseer of your souls. 1 Peter 2:25
- Just as Moses lifted up the **snake** in the wilderness, so the Son of Man must be lifted up. John 3:14
- What they trust in is fragile; what they rely on is a **spider**'s web. Job 8:14
- Benjamin is a ravenous **wolf**; in the morning he devours the prey, in the evening he divides the plunder. Genesis 49:27

Adam Taylor/DigitalVision/Thinkstock

Match Madness!

Want to kick it up a notch with a little extra challenge for older kids? Copy (only once!), cut, fold, and toss the following scripture verses into the hat. Players who get these clues have to pair up with the person who holds their animals' male/female counterparts rather than finding exact scripture matches.

- They exchanged their glorious God for an image of a **bull**, which eats grass. Psalm 106:20
- "Very well," he said, "I will let you bake your bread over **cow** dung instead of human excrement." Ezekiel 4:15
- Make for the tent a covering of **ram** skins dyed red, and over that a covering of the other durable leather. Exodus 26:14
- Abraham set apart seven **ewe** lambs from the flock. Genesis 21:28
- Come away, my beloved, and be like a gazelle or like a young **stag** on the spice-laden mountains. Song of Songs 8:14
- Even the **doe** in the field deserts her newborn fawn because there is no grass. Jeremiah 14:5
- Peter replied, "Man, I don't know what you're talking about!" Just as he was speaking, the **rooster** crowed. Luke 22:60
- Jerusalem, Jerusalem, you who kill the prophets and stone those sent to you, how often I have longed to gather your children together, as a **hen** gathers her chicks under her wings, and you were not willing. Matthew 23:37

WichitS/iStock/Thinkstock

Noah's Way!

Make Noah's ark, using basic origami and paper animal cutouts, by doing the Classic Sailboat activity in Chapter 10.

Birds of the Bible

Hand out copies of the following scripture list (opposite page) as a field guide for a bird-watching activity, challenging kids to see how many types of birds they can spot. Of course, some species are not indigenous to your area, so encourage kids to take note of other birds as well. If you want to add some depth to this exercise, before going out in the field, white-out the bird names in each scripture for a fill-in-the-blanks project (as in Chapter 1).

Look at the birds of the air; they do not sow or reap or store away in barns, and yet your heavenly Father feeds them. Are you not much more valuable than they?

Leviticus 6:4

For the Birds

Adorn a nearby tree or shrub with edible decor for your feathered friends. Simply collect some pinecones, string each with a piece of yarn, slather with peanut butter, and then roll in fresh birdseed or whole-grain bread crumbs. Hang them like you're decorating a Christmas tree, and finish off with a garland strung with air-popped popcorn (no butter or salt please) and fresh cranberries.

The Bible Adventure Book of Scavenger Hunts

Who Flew?

- Just as Jesus was coming up out of the water, he saw heaven being torn open and the Spirit descending on him like a **dove**. Mark 1:10

- Does the **eagle** soar at your command and build its nest on high? Job 39:27

- No bird of prey knows that hidden path, no **falcon**'s eye has seen it. Job 28:7

- Does the **hawk** take flight by your wisdom and spread its wings toward the south? Job 39:26

- Who gives the **ibis** wisdom or gives the **rooster** understanding? Job 38:36

- The wings of the **ostrich** flap joyfully, though they cannot compare with the wings and feathers of the **stork**. Job 39:13

- I am like a desert **owl**, like an owl among the ruins. Psalm 102:6

- Like a **partridge** that hatches eggs it did not lay are those who gain riches by unjust means. Jeremiah 17:11

- That evening **quail** came and covered the camp, and in the morning there was a layer of dew around the camp. Exodus 16:13

- Who provides food for the **raven** when its young cry out to God and wander about for lack of food? Job 38:41

- Like a fluttering **sparrow** or a darting **swallow**, an undeserved curse does not come to rest. Proverbs 26:2

- Wherever there is a carcass, there the **vultures** will gather. Matthew 24:28

Image Source White/Image Source/Thinkstock

Craft Fun! Be a Bird's BFF

Do a big—or pint-size—favor for your feathered friends! Use empty milk cartons (left over from activities in Chapter 4) and paints to make classic cardboard bird feeders.

1) Carefully use a sharp knife to cut a square in the front of the carton—an opening as little as 1 1/4 inch is enough for small birds to enter.
2) Take the tip of the knife to forge a smaller hole at the top to add a string for hanging.
3) Use flat acrylic craft paints to colorfully decorate feeder, letting dry completely between coats.
4) Fill with birdseed, and then clamp the top shut with a paperclip.
5) String up the completed bird feeder, and hang from a tree.

HotPhotoPie/iStock/Thinkstock

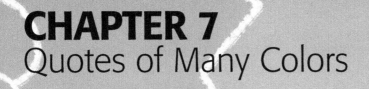

CHAPTER 7
Quotes of Many Colors

I have set my rainbow in the clouds, and it will be the sign of the covenant between me and the earth.

Genesis 9:13

Quotes of Many Colors

Because this scavenger hunt requires very little planning and preparation, it's a great impromptu activity—hey, perhaps for a rainy day. Bible-quoted color references challenge players to collect colorful objects before jumping into some rainbow-inspired projects.

Like the appearance of a rainbow in the clouds on a rainy day, so was the radiance around him.

Ezekiel 1:28

Nata_Snow/iStock/Thinkstock

A World of Color

Photocopy the list of scripture references that appears in the Color Coated project on the opposite page, so you have as many complete copies as players. Get deflated rubber balloons in an assortment of colors, and place one complete list, folded up, in each balloon before inflating. Players must pop the balloons to get to the lists and then look up all the verses.

Have kids search for items that correspond with the colors cited in the list of scriptures. This hunt can be played with teams, pairs, or individuals—game coordinator's choice. To make the game more difficult, ask players to bring back more than one item of each color. Afterward, kids use the same list of scripture references to decode the color-by-symbols activity.

Color Coated

Using the scripture-based key, crack the color-by-symbols code to fill in the ornate robe. Share the story of Joseph and his brothers, in Genesis 37, while coloring.

□ = Exodus 24:10   ☆ = Proverbs 20:29   ⬡ = Mark 9:3

O = Leviticus 13:36   △ = Song of Songs 5:11   ☩ = John 19:5

◇ = Job 39:8   ♡ = Matthew 16:2

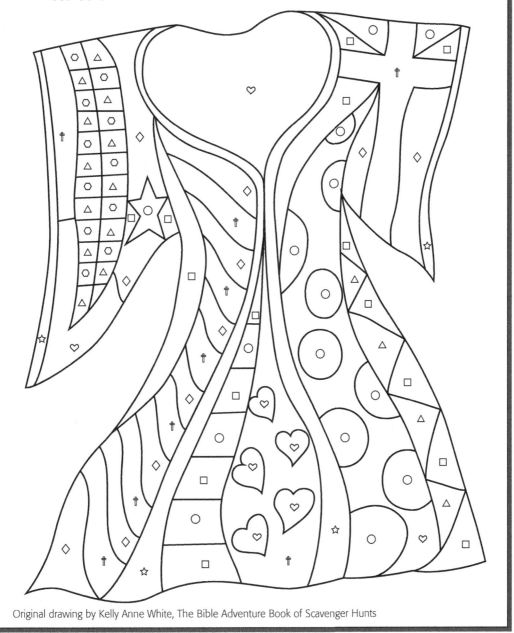

Original drawing by Kelly Anne White, The Bible Adventure Book of Scavenger Hunts

Israel loved Joseph more than any of his other sons,
because he had been born to him in his old age;
and he made an ornate robe for him.

Genesis 37:3

Answer Key: Color Coated

□ = Under his feet was something like a pavement made of lapis lazuli, as bright **blue** as the sky. Exodus 24:10

○ = The priest is to examine them, and if he finds that the sore has spread in the skin, he does not need to look for **yellow** hair. Leviticus 13:36

◇ = It ranges the hills for its pasture and searches for any **green** thing. Job 39:8

☆ = The glory of young men is their strength, **gray** hair the splendor of the old. Proverbs 20:29

△ = His head is like the finest gold; his locks are wavy, and **black** as a raven. Song of Songs 5:11

♡ = He replied, "When evening comes, you say, 'It will be fair weather, for the sky is **red**.'" Matthew 16:2

⬡ = His clothes became dazzling **white**, whiter than anyone in the world could bleach them. Mark 9:3

✝ = When Jesus came out wearing the crown of thorns and the **purple** robe, Pilate said to them, "Here is the man!" John 19:5

Ryan McVay/DigitalVision/Thinkstock

Science Project: Rainbow in a Bottle

Who says rainbows are for rainy days only? Make your own—no matter the weather!

What you need: glass bottle, water, light source, white sheet of paper

1) Fill a clear glass bottle or jar with water.
2) Place a sheet of paper on a flat surface such as the ground or on a table.
3) Hold the water jar up so the sunlight (or a flashlight or lamplight) hits it in such a way that a beam of light passes through the water.
4) Watch as colors are cast, from seven different wavelengths, onto the white sheet of paper.

David Morrison/Hemera/Thinkstock

The Hose Knows

Play around with the garden hose on a sunny day, perhaps while gardening (Chapter 3), by spraying at different angles to produce rainbows. What color of the rainbow is *not* mentioned in the Bible? Answer: orange.

Sky Light

In 2002, two astronomers deemed the color of the universe to be a light beige—hypothetically visible to the eye if all the light in the universe were contained at once. The Johns Hopkins University researchers nicknamed the color "Cosmic Latte," so the recipe below is for a caffeine-free latte inspired by that color.

Recipe

Not-of-This-World Latte

This is a wonderful warm beverage for enjoying on a chilly overcast day or at night underneath the stars.

15-ounce can pure pumpkin
1/4 cup smooth peanut butter
2 tablespoons pure honey

1 teaspoon ground cinnamon
2 quarts vanilla almond milk

Combine all the ingredients in a large saucepan over medium heat on a stove or over a campfire. Bring to a slow simmer, stirring often. Ladle warmed latte into heat-friendly cups or mugs, or let cool slightly and then serve over ice for an iced latte. Fancy it up! Top with fresh *whipped cream*, drizzle with pure *maple syrup*, and sprinkle on some *graham-cracker crumbs*. Makes 7 cups.

Too hot to handle? Make smoothies instead! Whisk the exact same ingredients in a large bowl, and then add to a blender in batches with some ice. Pour into cups with straws, and add the fancy toppings. The Bible Adventure Book of Scavenger Hunts

Liesel_Fuchs/iStock/Thinkstock

CHAPTER 8
What's Your Number?

*Your servant is here among the
people you have chosen, a great people,
too numerous to count or number.*

1 Kings 3:8

What's Your Number?

This is an early-morning player-elimination game that uses numerical scripture references as a countdown to rounds. It's also a sneaky way to spiff up the grounds and facilities since players who *Step Back* drop out of the game to do chores while *Saved* players move forward. Because of this game's nuances, it's best played in a church or camp setting.

- *This hunt is best for older kids* since it eliminates players and also requires the ability to perform cleaning tasks. Two players are eliminated right away, so be sure participants are mature enough to handle and are very clear on the rules.
- *The game challenges two teams,* each with 10 players (20 kids in all), with Bible-based numerical references, counting down from numbers 10 through 1. One player from each team drops off at every round of the game.
- *Play with fewer people* by picking up the game at a different round. For the elimination process to work, the number of members on each team must equal the number assigned to whichever round you start the game. For example, two teams of eight can begin the hunt with the *Saved* clues in round #8.
- *Teams receive the same sets of clues,* always placed in individual envelopes (one for each player) marked *Team A* and *Team B,* along with the number of the round the game is on, which should always match up to the number of players per team.
- *Mark outsides of envelopes with the corresponding clue number,* and leave them unsealed until you're ready to place in hiding spots so you can double-check the contents if needed. Be sure to read thoroughly through this entire scavenger hunt beforehand since it requires quite a bit of pre-planning.
- *Clues begin with these phrases: Step Back!* or *Saved!* Campers whose clues read *Step Back!* are eliminated in that round (hand them rubber gloves because they'll be cleaning). Those marked *Saved!* move on to the next phase of the game.
- *You'll need to stock up on a few things* for this game:
  - ❏ Bread
  - ❏ Cheese
  - ❏ Stationery
  - ❏ Envelopes
  - ❏ Rubber gloves
  - ❏ Plastic trumpets
  - ❏ String or yarn
  - ❏ Popsicle sticks
  - ❏ Invisible tape
  - ❏ Ring toss set
  - ❏ Coin
  - ❏ Two dozen donuts

Countdown Invitational

Forward the first set of clues to Teams A and B, so players (10 on each team) receive them in the morning. Clues consist of the following scripture verses (each of these needs to be written only once), prompting the two teams to meet up with each other for breakfast.

For Team A, deliver packages of sliced bread, along with the following scripture:

> *Take this ephah of roasted grain and these 10 loaves*
> *of bread for your brothers and hurry to their camp.*
> *1 Samuel 17:17*

For Team B, give packs of cheese slices, with this verse attached:

> *Take along these 10 cheeses to the commander of your*
> *brothers' unit. See how they are and bring back some*
> *assurance from them.*
> *1 Samuel 17:18*

Grilled Cheese, Please!

When the two teams meet up—one team bringing the bread and the other holding the cheese—explain the game to them over a grilled-cheese breakfast. Round out the meal with fresh fruits, nuts or bacon, and beverages. Of course, you don't have to dole out a literal 10 loaves of bread and cheese if it's more than you need to feed players, so use common sense, being sure you have enough for all. Consider using plastic food-storage bags to divvy up the bread and cheese before delivering it with the clues.

summersgraphicsinc/iStock/Thinkstock

> *To a larger group give a larger inheritance, and to a smaller group a smaller one; each is to receive its inheritance according to the number of those listed.*

Numbers 26:54

Note: During breakfast, while going over game rules, a game coordinator needs to secretly tuck envelopes bearing all of Command #8's clues into both team's bunks or lockers.

After breakfast, teams begin the search, based on the scripture postings (opposite page), for individual sealed envelopes containing the next clue. Explain that one player from each team will be eliminated—all in good fun!—at each stage of the game, beginning *now*.

chayathonwong/iStock/Thinkstock

Countdown Command #10

Inform players that they will receive 10 Countdown Commands, starting with the following two Bible verses, which are to be made to look like two stone tablets and posted in a visible area near the breakfast site.

allanswart/iStock/Thinkstock

He declared to you his covenant, the 10 Commandments, which he commanded you to follow and then wrote them on two stone tablets.

Deuteronomy 4:13

This is the Lord's sign to you that the Lord will do what he has promised: Shall the shadow go forward 10 steps, or shall it go back 10 steps?

2 Kings 20:9

Countdown Command #9

Ten steps *forward* from the stone-tablet postings, hide two envelopes (one marked *Team A*, and the other *Team B*) with the following scripture clue.

Step Back!

It was 9 in the morning when they crucified him.

Mark 15:25

What time is it? Time for you to drop out of the game, sorry! You and a member from the other team get to stay behind and clean up the breakfast mess while the rest of the campers move on to the next clue. Boo-hoo.

First clean the inside of the cup and dish,
and then the outside also will be clean.

Matthew 23:26

Jupiterimages/Pixland/Thinkstock

Ten steps *back* from the stone-tablet postings, stash 18 envelopes (nine for *Team A*, the other half for *Team B*) containing the following scripture-based clue.

Saved!

*The rest of the people cast lots to bring one out of every
ten of them to live in Jerusalem, the holy city, while the
remaining 9 were to stay in their own towns.*

Nehemiah 11:1

You're not in the holy city quite yet, but you're still in the game. Return to your "own-town" base, and check your bunk or locker for the next clue.

*Coming to his hometown, he began teaching the people in
their synagogue, and they were amazed. "Where did this man
get this wisdom and these miraculous powers?" they asked.*

Matthew 13:54

Countdown Command #8

Hand out pairs of rubber gloves at each round to players who have to *Step Back!* Players who are *Saved!* return to their cabins (or lockers), where they'll each find the next bunch of clues—randomly hidden during breakfast—in their bunks. If a player doesn't have a clue under her pillow or in her locker, she should take it from that of the player who was eliminated in the last round. Two envelopes, one marked for each *Team A* and *Team B*, contain the following clue, and are randomly shuffled in with the rest before hiding in bunks or lockers.

Step Back!

*To those who were disobedient long ago when God waited
patiently in the days of Noah while the ark was being built. In it
only a few people, 8 in all, were saved through water.*

1 Peter 3:20

Unfortunately you randomly scored the short Mount Ararat straw, left high-and-dry! Step back while the other eight in your team move up to the Mount of Olives. You and the opposing team's member will baptize the bathrooms with bubbly water because now you're on scrub-a-dub-tub duty (ew!).

PhotoEuphoria/iStock/Thinkstock

Sixteen envelopes, divided evenly between both teams, marked *A* or *B*, and tucked in players' bunks or lockers, have the following clue.

Saved!

"Truly I tell you, some who are standing here will not taste death before they see the kingdom of God." About 8 days after Jesus said this, he went up onto a mountain to pray. As he was praying, the appearance of his face changed, and his clothes became as bright as a flash of lightning.

Luke 9:27–29

Go to the top of the highest point of the grounds with your other team members for…silent prayer?

DigitalVision/Thinkstock

Countdown Command #7

At the top of a nearby hill, leave 16 inexpensive plastic toy trumpets (available from party suppliers) with sealed clues attached. Use a hole punch, and string or yarn, to secure envelopes to toys. Each player takes one trumpet, two of which have the following clue.

Step Back!

He will confirm a covenant with many for one '7.' In the middle of the '7' he will put an end to sacrifice and offering. And at the temple he will set up an abomination that causes desolation, until the end that is decreed is poured out on him.

Daniel 9:27

The end is decreed. Take seven short steps away from the rest of the players. Pair up with the other player who has stepped seven steps from the group.

Have 7 priests carry trumpets of rams' horns in front of the ark. On the 7th day, march around the city 7 times, with the priests blowing the trumpets.

Joshua 6:4

Today is the day you and a member of the other team march around the grounds seven times, trumpeting the virtues of a clean environment, as you bag up litter along the way. Thank you!

Purestock/Thinkstock

The remaining 14 trumpets have the following clue.

Saved!

*On the first day of the 7th month hold a sacred assembly and
do no regular work. It is a day for you to sound the trumpets.*
                                                    Numbers 29:1

Save the date—you're saved today. It's been decreed that you get to relax, so sound off!

*Then Peter came to Jesus and asked, "Lord, how many times shall
I forgive my brother or sister who sins against me? Up to 7 times?"
Jesus answered, "I tell you, not 7 times, but seventy-7 times."*
                                                    Matthew 18:21–22

Take 77 steps forward in the spirit of pure forgiveness to get to your next clue.

Countdown Command #6

In an area located 77 measured paces forward from the location of the last clue, place a pile of envelopes for players to randomly pluck from a makeshift "nest." Two envelopes, one each for Team A and Team B, have the following clue.

Ornitolog82/iStock/Thinkstock

Step Back!

Six of the towns you give the Levites will be cities of refuge, to which a person who has killed someone may flee.

Numbers 35:6

You'd kill to stay in the game? Um, thou shalt not kill. You've been chosen to take refuge. Take six steps backward, away from the group, and join the player from the other team who also takes six steps back.

The throne had 6 steps, and a footstool of gold was attached to it. On both sides of the seat were armrests, with a lion standing beside each of them.

2 Chronicles 9:18

As a demonstration of courage and commitment, you and the other player are to go to the person in charge of directing this game and ask to serve in a volunteer capacity, accepting any task he or she doles out.

A dozen envelopes, half marked *A* and the other half *B*, have the following clue.

Saved!

Then Balaam saw the Kenites and spoke his 6th message:
"Your dwelling place is secure, your nest is set in a rock."

Numbers 24:21

Your spot in this game is securely set in stone…for now.

Twelve lions stood on the 6 steps, one at
either end of each step. Nothing like it had
ever been made for any other kingdom.

2 Chronicles 9:19

There are twelve of you left in all, brave souls. Now the six of you on Team A are to take six sideways steps to the left, while the six on Team B take six steps to the right side.

Countdown Command #5

Six measured paces away on the right and left sides of the "nest," leave sacks containing the next batch of clues. Make two copies of the following clue, one to go in Team A's sack and the other for Team B.

Step Back!

To one he gave 5 bags of gold, to another two bags, and to another one bag, each according to his ability. Then he went on his journey. But the man who had received one bag went off, dug a hole in the ground and hid his master's money.

Matthew 25:15, 18

You've dug yourself into a hole, so you're now on wash-and-fold duty. Go with the other team's member to the laundry room, where you'll wash towels and linens, but first here's a quick lesson on how to fold:

Join 5 of the curtains together into one set and the other six into another set. Fold the sixth curtain double at the front of the tent.

Exodus 26:9

Make 10 copies of the following clue, five for each team.

Saved!

The man who had received 5 bags of gold went at once and put his money to work and gained 5 more.

Matthew 25:16

Score! You're golden, so here's your next clue:

Also make crossbars of acacia wood: 5 for the frames on one side of the tabernacle, 5 for those on the other side, and 5 for the frames on the west, at the far end of the tabernacle.

Exodus 26:26–27

You've been framed! Your next set of instructions can be found on the west end of the worship center, so step it up.

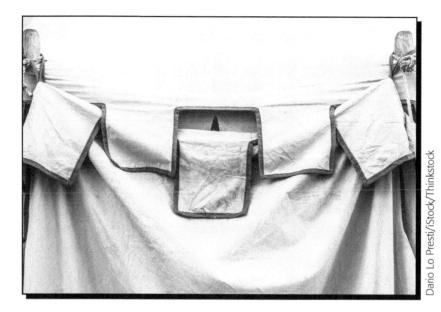

Dario Lo Presti/iStock/Thinkstock

Countdown Command #4

Glue Popsicle sticks to frame the envelopes that hold these clues, and securely tape them to the west-facing wall of the worship center for players to choose from at random. Post two of the following, one marked *A* and one marked *B*.

Step Back!

When the soldiers crucified Jesus, they took his clothes, dividing them into 4 shares, one for each of them, with the undergarment remaining. This garment was seamless, woven in one piece from top to bottom.

John 19:23

Things aren't always what they...seam. You and another player are to join the other two who are already on laundry duty.

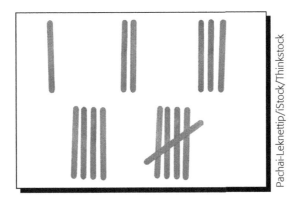

Pachai-Leknettip/iStock/Thinkstock

And post eight of these, four marked *A* and four marked *B*.

Saved!

*In my vision at night I looked, and there before me were the
4 winds of heaven churning up the great sea. Four great
beasts, each different from the others, came up out of the sea.*

Daniel 7:2–3

A dream come true? On to the next clue.

*The altar hearth is 4 cubits high, and 4 horns
project upward from the hearth.*

Ezekiel 43:15

Countdown Command #3

On an altar or mantel inside the worship center, place two containers (one for Team A, one for Team B) to hold "bouquets" of the next eight sealed envelopes, folded and taped into cone shapes. Make two copies of the following clue, marked *A* and *B*.

Step Back!

*"Truly I tell you," Jesus answered, "this very night, before
the rooster crows, you will disown me 3 times."*

Matthew 26:34

Game over. You've been disowned. Redeem yourself by checking in with the cook staff since you and another player are on kitchen patrol.

Make six copies of the following clue, three marked *A* and three *B*.

Saved!

*These 3 men, firmly tied, fell into the blazing
furnace. Then King Nebuchadnezzar leaped to his feet
in amazement and asked his advisers, "Weren't there 3
men that we tied up and threw into the fire?"*

Daniel 3:23–24

Things are heating up, but don't sweat it! You're still in the game.

*With 3 administrators over them, the satraps were made
accountable to them so that the king might not suffer loss.*

Daniel 6:2

*And now these 3 remain: faith, hope and love.
But the greatest of these is love.*

1 Corinthians 13:13

Go with your team of three to the administrative office to account for your next clue.

Countdown Command #2

At the administrative office, have just two copies of the following clue, one for each team of three, marked *A* and *B*.

Saved!

*Again, truly I tell you that if 2 of you on earth agree about anything
they ask for, it will be done for them by my Father in heaven.*
Matthew 18:19

Jesus is right-on! This game requires only two from each team to move on from here.

*Two are better than one, because they have a good
return for their labor: If either of them falls down, one can help
the other up. But pity anyone who falls and has no one to help
them up. Though one may be overpowered, 2 can defend
themselves. A cord of three strands is not quickly broken.*
Ecclesiastes 4:9–10, 12

How to decide who stays and who goes?

*Cast four gold rings for it and fasten them to its four
feet, with 2 rings on one side and 2 rings on the other.*
Exodus 25:12

Ring toss! Best two players out of three move on to the final countdown.

Pachai-Leknettip/iStock/Thinkstock

Move outdoors or to a spacious indoor area for the ring toss. Hand this clue, one marked *A* and one *B*, to the player on each team who scores lowest in the ring-toss challenge.

Step Back!

Ring toss? Your loss! Three's a crowd—in love, not war. Who's the boss? Find out your chore.

Countdown Command #1

Assign a chore of your choice to the players (one from each team), who lost the ring toss. Hand these identical envelopes to all four of the remaining players, two marked *A* and the other two *B*.

Saved!

This is good, and pleases God our Savior, who wants all people to be saved and to come to a knowledge of the truth. For there is 1 God and 1 mediator between God and mankind, the man Christ Jesus.

1 Timothy 2:3–5

Who won? Coin toss! Who prevails? Heads or tails.

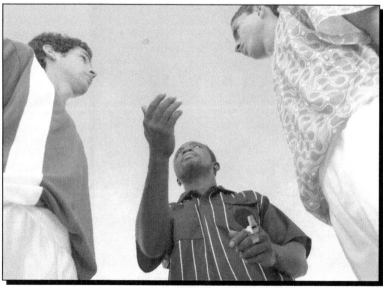

Mike Watson Images/moodboard/Thinkstock

Players compete in a coin toss, each against his own teammate, leaving only one player from Team A and one from Team B. The two players who lose the coin toss each receive an envelope containing this clue.

Step Back!

*Suppose a woman has ten silver coins and loses 1.
Doesn't she light a lamp, sweep the house
and search carefully until she finds it?*

Luke 15:8

Coin toss? Your loss! Grab a broom. Sweep some rooms.

Countdown Command #0

The game is now down to two final players, one from each team. Since "zero" is referenced nowhere in the Bible, the game circles back around to where it started (at number 10), continuing with double-digit figures as its closing theme. Place the final two verses in separate *unmarked* envelopes. Shuffle them up, and tape them to two dozen-count boxes of donuts, giving one box to each of the game's finalists. One envelope contains the verse below. Turn the page for the other envelope's verse.

Step Back!

*Do you think I cannot call on my Father, and he will at once
put at my disposal more than twelve legions of angels?*

Matthew 26:53

The angels have blessed you with a legion of one dozen donuts, but you drew the "11" card so you have to surrender one of your donuts to the countdown champ.

*"Listen" he said, "I had another dream, and this time the sun
and moon and 11 stars were bowing down to me."*

Genesis 37:9

It's your turn to bow down and serve. Take the remaining donuts, and dole them out to all your teammates for their hard work doing chores. One extra? It's yours!

The second envelope contains the following scripture reference. The player who receives this verse is the winner of the game!

Saved!

Take the finest flour and bake 12 loaves of bread,
using two-tenths of an ephah for each loaf.

Leviticus 24:5

Time to eat the donuts! You get a baker's dozen since the opposing team's final player has to forfeit one to you. And now it's your turn to serve. Take your 13 donuts, and dole them out to all your teammates for their hard work doing chores while you mastered the numbers game. Extra donuts? One for you, two to share with group leaders!

The Jews in Susa had assembled on the thirteenth and
fourteenth and then on the fifteenth they rested and
made it a day of feasting and joy.

Esther 9:18

Jupiterimages/Stockbyte/Thinkstock

They all ate and were satisfied, and the disciples picked up
twelve basketfuls of broken pieces that were left over.

Luke 9:17

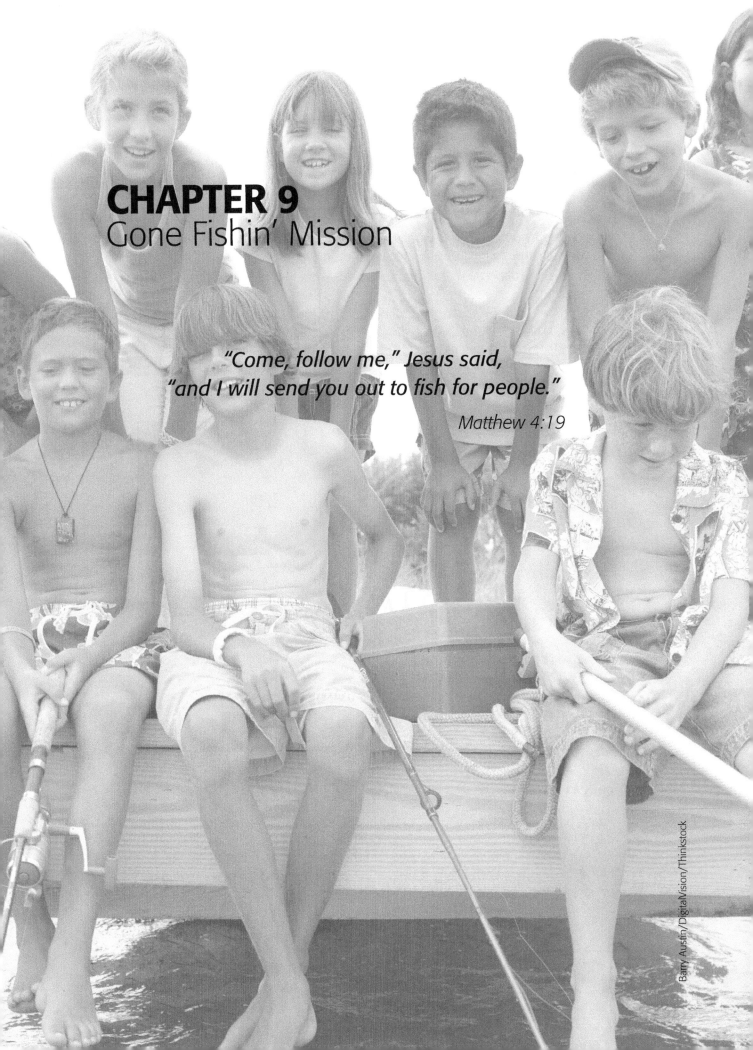

CHAPTER 9
Gone Fishin' Mission

"Come, follow me," Jesus said,
"and I will send you out to fish for people."

Matthew 4:19

Gone Fishin' Mission

This scavenger hunt uses biblical fishing references as clues, which players have to "fish" for around the grounds. Yep, some water is involved.

- *Count the number of kids* who will be playing, so you'll know how many copies of each scripture to print out. Every player gets a copy of each clue.
- *Number the opposite sides* of the fish so kids know they're finding clues in the correct sequence.
- *Start the game by posting an announcement* on a bulletin board: *Feel Like a Fish Outta Water? Join the Gone-Fishin' Mission!* Be sure to include details of the time and place the fun begins.
- *Once the game begins, tell campers to take note* of the one keyword in **bold** in each scripture that provides a clue as to the location of the next clue.

AleksandarDickov/iStock/Thinkstock

Clue #1

Attach paperclips to the "mouths" of the first clue's fish-shaped paper, and put them all into a large bowl or even a small kiddie pool that's *not* filled with water. Have kids tie a magnet to one end of a two-foot piece of fishing line and tie the other end of the string to the tip of a stick. Each player fishes for the scripture-based clue (opposite page). Tell players to toss 'em back if they catch more than one.

*Once again, the kingdom of heaven is like a **net** that was let down into the lake and caught all kinds of fish. When it was full, the fishermen pulled it up on the shore. Then they sat down and collected the good fish in baskets, but threw the bad away.*

Matthew 13:47–48

fotoember/iStock/Thinkstock

Clue #2

These clues are to be tucked into a volleyball **net**, so you might need more paperclips to secure. Make two different sets of clues, one for *bad fish* and one for *good fish* as instructed.

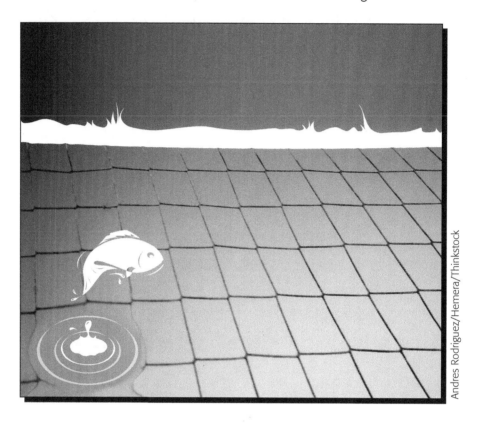

Andres Rodriguez/Hemera/Thinkstock

Bad Fish

Leave out a wastebasket labeled *Bad Fish* for players to throw away all the *bad* clues.

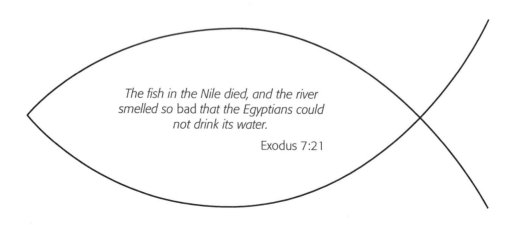

The fish in the Nile died, and the river smelled so bad *that the Egyptians could not drink its water.*

Exodus 7:21

Good Fish

After sorting all of the fish, players then follow the clue highlighted on the *good* fish.

*God created the great creatures of the sea and every living thing with which the **water** teems and that moves about in it, according to their kinds, and every winged bird according to its kind. And God saw that it was* good.

Genesis 1:21

Fuse/Thinkstock

Clue #3

This bunch of clues will float on a body of **water**, such as a swimming pool or clean lake—or even a large tub or utility sink. Roll up the pieces of fish-shaped paper that contain the scripture provided below, and place inside deflated rubber balloons. Blow up the balloons, and float them on the water's surface to mimic whales. Players must fish the balloons out of the water and then pop them to get to the next clue.

chezball/iStock/Thinkstock

*As Jonah was three days and three nights in the belly of a huge fish, so the Son of Man will be three days and three nights in the **heart** of the earth.*

Matthew 12:40

Clue #4

Use small rocks to make a large **heart** shape on the ground somewhere nearby. In the center of the heart, set the next pile of fish-shaped clues. Cover the pile of clues with more rocks to hide them or keep them from blowing away.

armiblue/iStock/Thinkstock

*Jesus said, "So that we may not cause offense, go to the lake and throw out your **line**. Take the first fish you catch; open its mouth and you will find a four-drachma coin. Take it and give it to them for my tax and yours."*

Matthew 17:27

Clue #5

Use clothespins to hang the next clues on a clothes***line***—near a lake, if possible—and include small round pieces of paper to resemble drachmas if desired.

Vaidas Bucys/iStock/Thinkstock

*Jesus appeared again to his disciples, by the Sea of Galilee. The disciples followed in the boat, towing the net full of fish, for they were not far from shore, about a **hundred yards**. When they landed, they saw a fire of burning coals there with fish on it, and some bread.*

John 21:1, 8–9

Clue #6

In an area that measures one **_hundred yards_** from the clothesline, leave an outdoor grill (lid closed) piled with dry charcoal (not burning, please) and fish "sandwiches," with fish-shaped clues clipped between folded pieces of paper cut to look like sliced bread.

BananaStock/Thinkstock

*Jesus said, "Have the people sit down." There was plenty of **grass** in that place, and they sat down (about five thousand men were there). Jesus then took the loaves, gave thanks, and distributed to those who were seated as much as they wanted. He did the same with the fish.*

John 6: 10–11

Clue #7

Leave the final set of clues in a **grass**y area near the grill, where players can sit and enjoy a snack. Have coolers of bottled water and baskets with seven loaves of bread to share. Place a large clear fishbowl filled with goldfish crackers, and tuck the last clues in with the crackers so kids have to, well, *fish* them out.

Elio Mazzacane/Hemera/Thinkstock

*He told the crowd to sit down on the **ground**.*
When he had taken the seven loaves and given thanks, he
broke them and gave them to his disciples to distribute to the people,
and they did so. They had a few small fish as well; he gave thanks for them
also and told the disciples to distribute them. The people ate
and were satisfied. Afterward the disciples picked up seven
basketfuls of broken pieces that were left over.
About four thousand were present.

Mark 8:6–9

Encourage campers to sit on the **ground**, say a blessing, and enjoy!

Catch of the Day

At this point you can move on to a group fishing activity, or turn this into a picnic lunch. Here are some ideas:

- *Instead of plain loaves of bread, have hoagies* filled with tuna-fish salad, along with the goldfish crackers.
- *Fire up that charcoal grill, and cook* a firm fish for kids to eat on their bread (also grilled, if desired)—yummy fish sandwiches. Pickles? Ketchup? Bring it!
- *Go fishin', and fry up your catch* over an open fire. Crushed goldfish crackers make a great breading for fish. Just dip scaled and cleaned fish in beaten egg, and then roll in crumbs to coat before frying about five minutes on each side in a hot buttered skillet.

rjlerich/iStock/Thinkstock

Go Fish!

If you're going fishing, make certain a skilled adult is supervising, and never go alone in unknown territory. Following are some basic safety guidelines:

- *Remove hook from line,* and store in tackle box when walking to and from the fishing spot.
- *Wear lifejackets* when fishing from a boat or if near deep water with strong currents.
- *Have a first-aid kit* handy in the event of an emergency.
- *Be very careful when worming* and also when removing caught fish—use pliers. Hooks are sharp!
- *Be sure no one is behind you* before casting your line. (Hats and sunglasses offer some protection from flying hooks.)
- *Do not leave tackle on the ground.* Someone could trip on supplies or step on a hook.
- *Consider fishing with nets,* but be mindful of water safety, particularly if wading in deep or strong waters.

Christopher Robbins/DigitalVision/Thinkstock

CHAPTER 10
Love Thy Neighbor

He answered, "'Love the Lord your God with all your heart and with all your soul and with all your strength and with all your mind'; and, 'Love your neighbor as yourself.'"

Luke 10:27

Love Thy Neighbor

In this hunt, the kids write the clues and pass them to neighboring players! Kids can work individually or in teams. Set up a beginning team, for example, starting with Group A and moving through alphabetically to Group B, C, and so on. This activity can be done leisurely and stretched out for a day, or it can be a time-pressured beat-the-clock activity—your choice.

Pay It…Foreword

Before beginning this game, gather some used-up books—old hymnals, faith magazines, worn-out devotionals, expired church bulletins—any faith-based publications you don't mind ripping some pages from, making sure there is at least one publication for each group. Give the whole pile of recycling to the first team in the rotation, as well as a stack of the following game instructions (one for each cabin or group) along with the directions for Handy Handmade Envelope (on following page) copied for players.

BananaStock/Thinkstock

The Bible Adventure Book of Scavenger Hunts

Love Thy Neighbor Game Rules

Phase #1: Free Delivery

Pick one publication from the recycling pile (and a copy of these game rules), and then deliver the remaining papers to the next team. Players are to take one, pass it to another team, and so on, until each group has a publication in its possession.

Phase #2: Fold and Hold

Each team is to thoughtfully leaf through its picked publication and choose a single tear-out page. Carefully rip the page out of the book, and use it to make an envelope (see Handy Handmade Envelope craft instructions).

Phase #3: Book Nook

After making the envelope, discreetly and stealthily put the book or magazine in a secret hiding spot somewhere around the grounds. Don't let opposing teams see where you're stashing it!

Phase #4: Write On!

Now, have a brainstorm session. On a blank piece of notebook paper, create a rhyming, rapping, sappy, slap-happy, or super-sentimental piece of prose that provides a clear-but-challenging riddle as to where the book is hidden. Fold up the clue, and place it in the handmade envelope.

Phase #5: Seal the Deal

Once the envelope is stuffed, give the sealed clue to the same team or player that delivered the pile of books and magazines to your team so you're passing back now in the opposite direction. The first team to receive the publications should give its clue to the last team that received the pile.

Phase #6: Paper Chase

And the search is on! Crack the riddles to find the book that goes with each missing page that's been folded into an envelope. When all of the books have been collected, meet up for some paper-recycling projects.

Craft Fun! Handy Handmade Envelope

For each envelope, choose a page that provides additional clues to help players know what publication they're looking for.

1) Carefully rip the page from the publication, and place it on a flat surface.
2) Fold the two top corners down until their tips meet, as if you're making a paper airplane, and crease the paper at both diagonal folds.
3) Fold the bottom right corner up until the edge of the paper horizontally meets the edges of the other two flaps, and crease the diagonal fold.
4) Now flip the paper over so all the flaps are facing your work surface, turning so the pointy end is up and the shortest straight edge is nearest you.
5) Fold the bottom edge up until you see a triangular flap that centers your envelope, and crease the bottom fold about a half inch from the point of the flap.
6) Pull the remaining paper down from the top right, tuck into your envelope, and crease.

More Craft Fun! Upcycled Paper Extravaganza

Wait! Don't toss all of those used books onto the recycling pile just yet. Following are some projects in which you upcycle the paper.

Classic Sailboat

Turn sailboats into arks by adding cutouts of animal pairs; fold paper in half before cutting silhouettes (Chapter 6 has a scripture list of animals in the Bible).

1) Fold an 8 1/2-by-11-inch piece of paper in half lengthwise and crease; unfold.
2) Fold in half again, this time from top to bottom, making a crease and keeping the paper folded.
3) From the horizontal folded edge, bring the top right and left corners down diagonally to meet in the center crease.
4) Fold up the bottom inch-wide strips on both sides of the paper.
5) Diagonally fold down all four corners of the strips so they become part of the triangle.
6) Open the triangle, and close it the other way so the two corners meet and make a square.
7) Fold both open-ended corners up on both sides of the paper to now form a smaller triangle than the first one.
8) Again, open the bottom of the triangle, pulling the two corners together and closing it to form a square.
9) Turn the square at an angle so it's like a diamond, the closed corner pointing up.
10) Gently pull out the sides of the two folds that meet at that corner, pulling the center triangle up as a "sail" and pushing the sides down so the body of the boat scoops in.

Number-One Fan

A pair of Popsicle sticks and a few book pages just might be the ticket to keeping cool in hot weather. Who knew?

1) Glue overlapped ends of Popsicle sticks to form a large L-shape; let dry completely.
2) Take a 5-by-15-inch sheet of paper (cut and glue two sheets together if necessary to make the correct size), and make a one-inch fold on one end.
3) Continue to fold, accordion-style, until the entire sheet is folded and creased.
4) Glue one end of the paper to the flat side of one of the glued Popsicle sticks, and do the same with the other end to the second stick.
5) Gather the loose folds, and secure in the center with a single staple or paperclip.
6) Let glue dry completely before fanning off.

Prayer Beads

Paper beads crafted from old hymnal pages or prayer books are great for making friendship bracelets. Love thy neighbor, right?

1) Cut paper from salvaged books or magazines into long triangular-shaped strips, playing around with different lengths and widths to create various sizes of beads.
2) Starting from the widest end, tightly roll the strips up around toothpicks or skewers.
3) When finished rolling, add a dab of glue to the triangle's tip to secure the bead.
4) Slide the bead off the toothpick, and let dry.
5) When you have enough beads, string them onto a piece of elastic and then tie a knot to secure.

Stockbyte/Thinkstock

Recycled Paper Projects…Continued!

Here are some other cool reasons for hitting up the paper recycling pile:

- *Shred it into confetti* for the end-of-session party (Chapter 12: Time to Part-ay!).
- *Make bookmarks* by cutting into panels; hole-punch the tops and add ribbon.
- *Create amazing collages.* Cover notebooks, lunchboxes, even shoe boxes.
- *Do papier-mâché projects,* using inflated balloons as molds—limitless options!
- *Wrap birthday gifts* in Sunday comics, magazine pages, or brown paper bags.

Jupiterimages/Creatas/Thinkstock

CHAPTER 11
Hidden Treasure Hunt

For where your treasure is,
there your heart will be also.

Luke 12:34

Hidden Treasure Hunt

For this hunt, you (or a group leader who has the best artistic skills) will need to draw a treasure map. Players use the map as a field guide to find hidden treasures around the campground or church grounds. Don't worry—you don't have to be a trained cartologist. You can make the map as ornate as you like but, ultimately, it's simple. Promise!

Jupiterimages/Creatas/Thinkstock

- *Read the game's instructions* since you'll need to pick up props and supplies to "bury" along the treasure-hunt route. Have enough so every player is able to collect pirate booty since, after the hunt, some of the supplies are used to make a kaleidoscope—one that looks like a pirate's spyglass (please also thoroughly read craft instructions for Pirate's Spyglass Kaleidoscope, near the end of this chapter).

- *Use an existing map of the grounds,* if one is available, as a base and draw on top of that. Otherwise, make a sketch of the area's general layout, drawing so it's accurate as far as north, south, east, and west. Read the clues first, so you'll know where to hide treasures and where to mark them on your map.

- *Draw small spot illustrations on the map,* based on specific keywords. For example, if gemstones are hidden in the garden, sketch small flowers and diamond shapes on that part of the map.

- *Use dotted lines and arrows on the map* to direct campers in the correct sequence. Make a *Start Here* point, and of course an *X* marks the spot where the final treasure is hidden.

- *Roll the map up, securely tie it, and put it in a corked bottle,* giving it to players to start the game. Assign one player as "keeper of the map" since this hunt is designed to be carried out as a group. You need to provide only one copy of the map and each piece of posted scripture for every group of players.

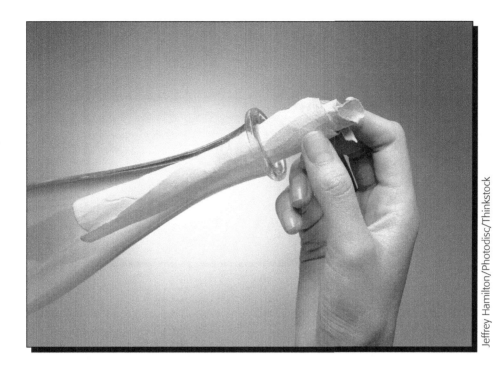

Jeffrey Hamilton/Photodisc/Thinkstock

Very Buried Treasure

Hide the clues around the grounds based on *suggested areas* marked in *italics*, along with **corresponding treasures** emphasized in **bold** (use bolded items as a guide for your shopping list of this game's supplies). You can shift the order to accommodate your route, but it might be fun to make players zigzag around the area. Just be sure to end the game with the last clue listed, and mark all the spots clearly since the map is the players' only clue as to the treasures' whereabouts. Players will need totes since they gather craft supplies along the way. The first few clues lead to bandannas and eye patches, which kids get to wear in the spirit of the hunt's pirate theme.

Treasure #1

In the *camp store* (or your church's thrift shop), set out a stack of **bandannas** in turquoise, purple, coral, and ruby colors for kids to tie around their heads like pirates. Above the stack, post a sign with the following words and scripture.

Sail! Today Only

*They exchanged turquoise, purple fabric, embroidered work,
fine linen, coral and rubies for your merchandise.*

Ezekiel 27:16

Wavebreakmedia Ltd/Thinkstock

Treasure #2

At the end of the swimming pool's plank (er, *diving board*), set a sack of **eye patches** (you can get them by the dozens from party suppliers, or make your own by simply cutting oval shapes from felt, then folding and gluing over thin elastic headbands). No pool? A large piece of scrap lumber placed on the ground will do the trick. Post the following sign nearby.

Walk the Plank

Can the blind lead the blind? Will they not both fall into a pit?
Why do you look at the speck of sawdust in your brother's eye
and pay no attention to the plank in your own eye?

Luke 6:39, 41

David De Lossy/Photodisc/Thinkstock

Treasure #3

In a section of the area where there are *gates*, hang strings of **fake pearls** (available from party suppliers) and post this sign with scripture.

The Pearly Gates

The twelve gates were twelve pearls, each gate made of a single pearl. The great street of the city was of gold, as pure as transparent glass.

Revelation 21:21

roman023/iStock/Thinkstock

Treasure #4

In the *lost-and-found* box, break open a roll or two of **pennies**. Post the following sign above the box.

Nothing Lost, Nothing Gained

A poor widow came and put in two very small copper coins, worth only a few cents. Calling his disciples to him, Jesus said, "Truly I tell you, this poor widow has put more into the treasury than all the others. They all gave out of their wealth; but she, out of her poverty, put in everything—all she had to live on."

Mark 12:42–44

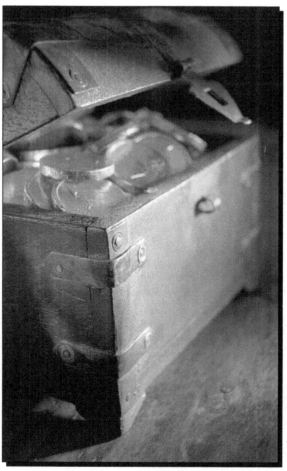

Monkey Business Images/Thinkstock

Treasure #5

In a *garden* or patch of wildflowers, plant colored fake **gemstones** (available from craft stores), either buried shallowly in the ground or scattered about for kids to collect. Post the following sign nearby.

En Garde-n

You were in Eden, the garden of God;
every precious stone adorned you: carnelian, chrysolite
and emerald, topaz, onyx and jasper, lapis lazuli, turquoise
and beryl. Your settings and mountings were made of gold;
on the day you were created they were prepared.

Ezekiel 28:13

TaiChesco/iStock/Thinkstock

Treasure #6

Against a *wall*, stack full-size **boxes of cereal** (shop warehouse stores for bulk packaging, one box for every four players, and choose varieties that fit with the game's nautical pirate theme). The cereal is for players to snack on, but also to use the boxes for triangular support strips to go inside kaleidoscopes (see craft instructions). Hang the following scripture on the wall.

Blimey! Bulkhead

The wall was made of jasper, and the city of pure gold, as pure as glass. The foundations of the city walls were decorated with every kind of precious stone.

Revelation 21:18–19

iqoncept/iStock/Thinkstock

Treasure #7

In the *worship center*, leave one full roll each of **plastic wrap** and **aluminum foil** (gold foil, too, if desired), as well as empty cardboard **paper-towel rolls** (one for each player in the group). Leave the following sign.

Fire in the Hole!

They burned the whole city and everything in it,
but they put the silver and gold and the articles of bronze
and iron into the treasury of the Lord's house.

Joshua 6:24

iqoncept/iStock/Thinkstock

Treasure #8

In a *field*, leave a photocopy of the Pirate's Spyglass Kaleidoscope craft instructions (on opposite page) and remaining supplies—**clear plastic sheets or containers**, **paper bags**, **rubber bands**, and **tape**—in a makeshift treasure chest (design one out of a cardboard box). Nearby, perhaps on a picnic table, have a station where kids can make their kaleidoscopes. Post the following sign near the "buried treasure."

Final Coffer(ing)

The kingdom of heaven is like treasure hidden in a field.
When a man found it, he hid it again, and then in his joy
went and sold all he had and bought that field.

Matthew 13:44

pioneer111/iStock/Thinkstock

Craft Fun! Pirate's Spyglass Kaleidoscope

What you need: flimsy plastic container or sheet, paper towel roll, marker, scissors, plastic wrap, thin rubber bands, fake gemstones, ruler, empty cereal box, aluminum foil, invisible tape, brown paper bag, hole punch

1) Take a flimsy plastic container—the kind baked goods or berries come in—or sheet of plastic (in craft stores) and trace a circle using the end of a paper towel roll.

2) Use the scissors to cut the circle, just inside the marked lines, from the plastic.

3) Place a small piece of plastic wrap at the end of the paper towel roll, pull tight, and secure with a rubber band.

4) Drop a small amount of fake gemstones into the roll—not too much since you want them to move around.

5) Drop the plastic circle into the roll, and use a ruler to gently flatten onto top of gems. Do not turn roll upside down at this point—your gems will spill out!

6) Place the ruler inside the tube and take a measurement.

7) Cut three 1 1/4-inch-wide strips of cardboard from cereal boxes to match the length just measured.

8) Cover cardboard strips in aluminum foil, shiny side facing out, and secure with tape on one side of each.

9) Tape the three foil-covered strips together, tape sides out, to form a triangular tube.

10) Slip the triangular tube inside the paper towel roll.

11) Cut a small brown-paper square to cover the open end of the roll, punching a hole in the center of the square, and secure with a thin rubber band.

12) Wrap remaining brown paper around the paper towel roll to cover, securing with tape.

13) Take three strips of aluminum foil, and fold them over lengthwise several times to form sturdy bands. Wrap one band around the center of the spyglass, using tape to secure, and the other two at the very edges around both ends of the roll. Now take a peek.

Jupiterimages/BananaStock/Thinkstock

Science Project: Shiny Doubloons

This inexpensive experiment uses certain food products to show how acids dissolve copper oxide to spiff up the pennies your pirates collected.

What you need: taco sauce, vinaigrette, pickle juice, lemonade, pennies, water

1) Set out a snack of corn chips and taco sauce, fresh veggies with vinaigrette for dipping, jars of sliced pickles, and pitchers of fresh-squeezed lemonade. Yes, that's right—time for munchies!

2) Now, in four separate small containers to be used for the experiment, pour some of the taco sauce, vinaigrette, pickle juice, and lemonade—*not* for consumption.

3) Have kids place their pennies in all four containers with the acidic foods, and let sit at least 10 minutes or more until pennies turn shiny and clean. Take note of which acids work fastest and best.

4) Discard the used liquids, and thoroughly rinse pennies in water so they maintain their shine—at least for a while. The copper will react to the air and slowly tarnish again over time.

Thoughts for Your Pennies...

Hey, penny pinchers! Here are 10 fun things you can do with those spare pennies that are hanging out in the far reaches of your pockets...

1. *Super-glue pennies to the bottoms of an old pair of shoes* at the toes and heels...and then do a little tap dance!
2. *Place a white piece of paper on top* of a penny, and rub it with a lead pencil to make an impression of the coin's image.
3. *Make a mosaic, using pennies* and other coins, by gluing to old plates or pieces of wood. Stretch the imagination!
4. *Trace a checkerboard or tic-tac-toe grid* into the dirt or sand, and use pennies as game pieces. One player has heads, the other tails.
5. *Challenge kids to a penny toss!* Just set out empty containers, Hula-Hoops, or upside-down Frisbees as targets, and let the games begin.
6. *Invent your own scavenger hunt,* one that requires players to follow trails of pennies to get to clues.
7. *Wire-wrap pennies, and use them on a hanging mobile* project (see Nature's Hang-up in Chapter 1).
8. *Decoupage-glue a tiny image* cut from a magazine—anything that inspires!—to a penny, and save it as a token reminder of God's love.
9. *Place some pennies at the bottom of a Mason jar,* and drop in a votive candle for a copper-accented glow.
10. *Put on a talent show,* and charge only penny admission!

sbeagle/iStock/Thinkstock

Make a Wish!

Toss shiny bright pennies into the campfire at night, and watch the copper turn the flames to colorful shades of blue and green.

Set the empty pot on the coals till it becomes hot and its copper glows, so that its impurities may be melted and its deposit burned away.

Ezekiel 24:11

David De Lossy/Photodisc/Thinkstock

CHAPTER 12
Time to Part-*ay!*

*Finally, brothers and sisters, rejoice!
Strive for full restoration, encourage one
another, be of one mind, live in peace. And
the God of love and peace will be with you.*

2 Corinthians 13:11

Time to Part-*ay!*

Designed to be played near the end of a youth group or camping session, all of this hunt's clues lead to different elements of party-planning—decorations, food, music, what-to-wear, when and where—all adding up to an invite to the farewell party, which will be held *that* night. Most of the clues are pre-packed in containers (empty five-quart ice cream buckets work great!) that are hidden around the campground or churchyard, so campers do not need any toting supplies. Instruct players, who will hunt together in a group, to take each bucket of clues along with them at each step of the game. So you can easily spot them for your shopping list, party supplies are highlighted in **bold**.

Fuse/Thinkstock

Clue #1

Start with a stack of **party hats**, one for each camper, with the following clue and scripture pasted on the insides of the hats. Consider posting an arrow nearby that points to the girls' and boys' restrooms since that's where the next clue will be hidden.

This pointy hat is just for you
It's pointing to your first big clue:
So when a camper's on the go,
Sometimes a camper's got to, um...*go* →

*If you point these things out to the brothers
and sisters, you will be a good minister of
Christ Jesus, nourished on the truths of the faith
and of the good teaching that you have followed.*

1 Timothy 4:6

Clue #2

Above buckets marked *Please Take One* and filled with **costume-jewelry pearls** and **discount-store neckties**, post the following sign in the girls' and boys' restrooms.

> Yes, good for you!
> Here's a new clue.
> Ties for the guys,
> Pearls for the girls

Include the following scripture on the boys' room sign.

> *I led them with cords of human kindness, with ties of love.*
> *Hosea 11:4*

Post this verse on the girls' room sign.

> *The kingdom of heaven is like a*
> *merchant looking for fine pearls.*
> *Matthew 13:45*

uriy2007/iStock/Thinkstock

Clue #3

To the buckets of pearls and ties, attach the following clue.

> Here's what-to-wear,
> Now where, oh, where?
> Keep on, it seems,
> Where streamers stream…
>
> *In the Lord's hand the king's heart is a stream of water that he channels toward all who please him.*
>
> *Proverbs 21:1*

Clue #4

Near a stream or other small body of water (use a sink or tub if you're a landlubber), leave a bucket filled with brand-new rolls of **blue, purple, and red party streamers**, with the following clue taped inside the lid of the bucket.

> OK, now where?
> Place of deep prayer…
> If you do care,
> Time to go there.
>
> *For the entrance to the tent make a curtain of blue, purple and scarlet yarn and finely twisted linen— the work of an embroiderer.*
>
> *Exodus 26:36*

Mike Watson Images/moodboard/Thinkstock

Clue #5

Leave a container of party **noisemakers** in the chapel or worship center with the following clue attached.

Shhh…quiet please,
No noise in here.
Head to the south
To yell and cheer!

What you'll find there?
Something higher
When it has air.
No, not a tire.

The camps on the south are to set out.
The blast will be the signal for setting out.
To gather the assembly, blow the trumpets.
Numbers 10:6–7

Fuse/Thinkstock

Clue #6

In a part of the camp located south from the worship center, leave a bunch of brand-new **rubber balloons**, with only one balloon inflated and tied to the bucket's handle. Players have to pop it to get to the following clue, which is tucked inside the balloon.

> Blow some more air,
> But not right now.
> Grab these balloons,
> And take a bow.
>
> You're doing great
> So celebrate.
> But do please wait;
> Don't yet inflate.
>
> Now, don't be late;
> It's time to move
> Into the wild—
> Get with the groove.
>
> *What did you go out into the wilderness to see?*
> *A reed swayed by the wind?*
>
> *Luke 7:24*

kreinick/iStock/Thinkstock

Clue #7

Hide the next bucket in a wooded or reedy area, filled with **confetti** and the following clue taped on the lid.

Are you ready
To throw confetti?
Please not yet
'Cause you can bet

That your next clue
Is close to you,
Not far from here
So have no fear.

Do not throw away your confidence; it will be richly rewarded.

Hebrews 10:35

Fuse/Thinkstock

Clue #8

Slightly deeper into the same wooded area, stash a bucket of art supplies—**pens**, **markers**, **watercolors**, **paints**, and **brushes**—and some **tape**, too, along with the following clue and scripture.

Having fun?
Almost done.
God wrote you
Another clue

On your heart.
Soon to part?
Don't be blue;
He loves you.

Look nearby,
Eagle eye,
Huge white roll
Like a scroll.

For we do not write you anything
you cannot read or understand. And
I hope that, as you have understood us
in part, you will come to understand fully
that you can boast of us just as we will
boast of you in the day of the Lord Jesus.

2 Corinthians 1:13–14

smiltena/iStock/Thinkstock

Clue #9

In the same wooded area, stash a large rolled-up sheet of **banner paper** with a ribbon wrapped around it. Once it's unrolled, kids will see this next clue and scripture written on the banner.

Quickly read,

Roll up again.

Take the lead…

What?

Where?

When?

Let him lead me to the banquet hall,
and let his banner over me be love.

Song of Songs 2:4

LuckyBusiness/iStock/Thinkstock

Clue #10

In a dining area or rec hall, have a tray of **cupcakes** waiting (see FROG Cupcakes sidebar at the end of this chapter), at least two for each player, and the following clue posted nearby.

> Take one cake now,
> Leave one for later.
> Right now, you are
> The decorator.
> (No, not the cake
> For heaven's sake!)
>
> Take all your décor
> To the party site.
> Surprise! Surprise!
> BIG bash tonight!
>
> *The sorrow was turned into joy and their*
> *mourning into a day of celebration.*
>
> *Esther 9:22*

Fuse/Thinkstock

Party Prep!

Direct everyone to go to the party's venue, and tell them to use all the supplies they gathered to decorate the place.

- *Use tape to hang streamers;* fill balloons with confetti (a funnel will help) and then inflate; paint and draw amazing artwork and messages on the blank side of the banner.
- *Spin a pre-party set of tunes* (see suggested Party Playlist on next page) to get party planners pumped.
- *Serve a snack of grapes* and beverages (see Fruit Loopy Fun Punch recipe on following page) so thirsty kids can have a drink—and also help fill ice trays with sparkling water and fruit to freeze for the punch.
- *After decorating, everybody can go rest up* and then get dressed up. Party attire? Pearls and ties required.

shironosov/IStock/Thinkstock

Put It on Your Playlist!

Need ideas for music downloads? Following is a list of some great dance party tunes by Christian sound artists:

- "Clap Your Hands" Audio Adrenaline
- "Welcome to the Show" Britt Nicole
- "Church Music (Dance!)" David Crowder Band
- "Up All Night" DJ Maj
- "Dance" The Katinas
- "Here to Party" LA Symphony
- "Jump" Lecrae
- "Spin" Lincoln Brewster
- "Dancefloor" Manic Drive
- "The Real Party (Trevon's Birthday)" Mary Mary
- "Dancing Generation" Matt Redman
- "Woo Hoo" Newsboys
- "Rock the Show" Paul Wright
- "Alive" Rebecca St. James
- "Already Over" Red
- "Sadie Hawkins Dance" Relient K
- "Say Goodbye" Sanctus Real
- "Boogie Bounce" Shonlock
- "Live Out Loud" Steven Curtis Chapman
- "Rock What You Got" Superchick
- "Get This Party Started" tobyMac
- "Insomniac" Trip Lee

maxoidos/iStock/Thinkstock

Recipe

Fruit Loopy Fun Punch

This recipe makes 26 cups of punch—plenty for your party!

- 1-liter bottle cherry-flavored sparkling water
- 64-ounce bottle white grape juice
- 46-ounce can pineapple juice
- 2-liter bottle ginger ale

Pour sparkling water into ice trays and freeze (for extra fun, drop grapes into each cube as in Chapter 3). Chill the remaining three ingredients in refrigerator before pouring into a large punch bowl, and then add sparkling ice cubes. Cheerio!

The Bible Adventure Book of Scavenger Hunts

They all ate the same spiritual food and drank the same spiritual drink; for they drank from the spiritual rock that accompanied them, and that rock was Christ.

1 Corinthians 10:3–4

Wiktory/iStock/Thinkstock

Fully-Rely-On-God (FROG) Cupcakes

Have fun decorating cupcakes to look like frogs' faces by first frosting with green-colored icing. For eyes, place white life-ring candies dotted with mini chocolate chips—use icing as "glue." Set the candy rings on their sides on tops of cupcakes so centers are facing forward. Make mouths with red licorice string. Ribbit!

David Gallaher/Hemera/Thinkstock

And so we know and rely on the love God has for us. God is love.
Whoever lives in love lives in God, and God in them.

1 John 4:16

About the Author

Kelly Anne White is author of *The Legend of the Fairy Stones* (Spring 2019). Kelly is an instructor for The PEN Institute and also a lesson designer on SchoolhouseTeachers.com, where you can find more of her scavenger hunt activities. As a former freelancer for HarperCollins Christian Publishing, she contributed to the *It's a Fact: Wacky Bible* series and many other books for middle-graders. Prior to her focus on book publishing, Kelly spent 15 years near the tippy-top of the masthead of *Girls' Life* magazine as senior executive editor. Following that stint, she served as editor-in-chief of several award-winning and globally syndicated websites. Kelly's Groovy Jesus poster line is available at etsy. com/shop/JesusPosters, which consists of designs based on pages from her upcoming *Jesus Groupie* series of books.